LAND O LAKES

™

CLASSIC COOKIES, BAKING & MORE

PUBLICATIONS INTERNATIONAL, LTD.

Recipes developed and tested by the Land O'Lakes Test Kitchens.
Recipes © 1991 Land O'Lakes, Inc.

Photo credits: Sanders Studio, Inc. Chicago, IL

ISBN: 1-56173-350-4

This edition published by:
Publications International, Ltd.
7373 North Cicero Avenue
Lincolnwood, Illinois 60646

Printed and bound in USA

8   7   6   5   4   3   2   1

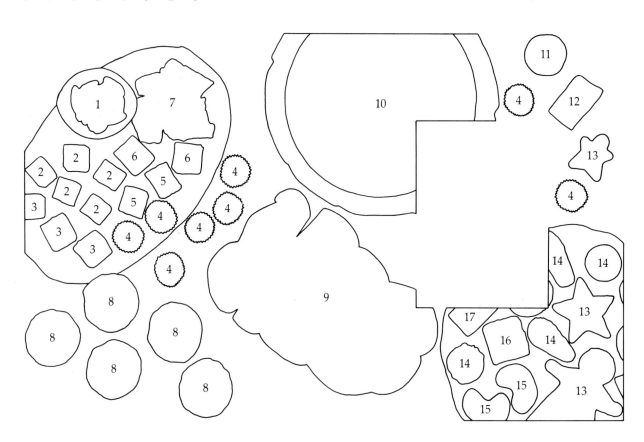

Pictured on the front and back cover:

1. Sugar & Spice Pecans (page 62)
2. Napoleon Crèmes (page 66)
3. Buttery Pecan Caramels (page 68)
4. Creamy Nut Dipped Candies (page 62)
5. Macadamia Nut Fudge (page 82)
6. Rocky Road Fudge (page 82)
7. Buttery Peanut Brittle (page 68)
8. Sparkling Cranberry Muffins (page 24)
9. Apricot Cardamom Wreath (page 80)

10. Chocolate Raspberry Torte (page 48)
11. Maple-Nut Cookies (page 32)
12. Fudgy Rocky Road Brownies (page 34)
13. Orange Spiced Gingerbread Cutouts (page 70)
14. Holiday Chocolate Butter Cookies (page 72)
15. Chocolate-Dipped Crescents (page 28)
16. Old-World Raspberry Bars (page 38)
17. Apricot Oatmeal Bars (page 38)

CONTENTS

SNACKS & APPETIZERS

BAKED BRIE WRAPPED IN PASTRY

This warm and creamy appetizer can be paired with crisp, sliced apples.

¾ cup all-purpose flour
¼ cup LAND O LAKES® Butter,
   softened
 1 package (3 ounces) cream
   cheese, softened
 1 round (8 ounces) Brie cheese
   (4¼-inch diameter)

1 egg
1 teaspoon water
  Apple slices
  Crackers

In large mixer bowl combine flour, butter and cream cheese. Beat at low speed, scraping bowl often, until mixture forms a dough, 2 to 3 minutes; shape into ball. Wrap tightly in plastic wrap; refrigerate, 30 to 60 minutes.

Heat oven to 400°. Divide pastry in half. On lightly floured surface, roll out *each* half of dough to ⅛-inch thickness. Cut a 7-inch circle from *each* half. Place one circle on cookie sheet. Place Brie cheese on center of pastry circle and top with other pastry circle. Pinch edges of pastry to seal. Flute edges as desired. Decorate top with small pastry cut-outs. In small bowl beat egg with water; brush over top and sides of pastry. Bake for 15 to 20 minutes or until golden brown. Remove from cookie sheet immediately. Let stand 30 minutes to allow cheese to set. Cut into small wedges and serve with apple slices and crackers.

Makes 8 servings

Baked Brie Wrapped in Pastry

EMPANADAS

A Southwestern favorite—sausage, egg, olives and raisins are combined in a pastry for a sure-to-please zesty appetizer.

CRUST
  2 cups all-purpose flour
  ¼ teaspoon salt

  ⅔ cup LAND O LAKES® Butter
  4 to 6 tablespoons cold water

FILLING
  ½ pound ground sausage
  1 cup chunky picante sauce
  ¼ cup chopped ripe olives
  ¼ cup raisins (optional)
  1 egg, hard-cooked, peeled, chopped

  ½ teaspoon garlic powder
  1 egg, slightly beaten
  Additional picante sauce

Heat oven to 425°. For crust, in large bowl combine flour and salt. Cut in butter until crumbly; with fork mix in just enough water to form a ball. Divide dough in half. Wrap in plastic wrap; set aside.

For filling, in 10-inch skillet cook sausage over medium heat, stirring occasionally, until crumbly and browned, 6 to 8 minutes. Drain fat. Add 1 cup picante sauce. Continue cooking, stirring occasionally, until sauce thickens slightly, 5 to 6 minutes. Add olives, raisins, hard-cooked egg and garlic powder. Continue cooking, stirring occasionally, until well mixed, 1 to 2 minutes. Set aside.

On lightly floured surface, shape *each* half of dough into 15-inch log. Roll *each* log into 20×5-inch rectangle. Cut *each* rectangle into 8 (5×2½-inch) rectangles. On one side of *each* rectangle place *about 1 tablespoon* of filling mixture. Brush edges of dough with water. Fold opposite side of dough over filling mixture; pinch edges together. With fork press to seal edges. Brush with beaten egg. Cut "X" in top of *each* empanada. Place empanadas on ungreased cookie sheets. Bake for 14 to 20 minutes or until lightly browned. Serve with additional picante sauce. *Makes 16 appetizers*

CONFETTI MUSHROOMS

These mushroom caps are stuffed with colorful vegetables.

  ¼ cup LAND O LAKES® Butter, melted
  ½ cup finely chopped carrot (1 medium)
  ¼ cup finely chopped green pepper

  2 tablespoons finely chopped onion
  ¼ cup dried crumbly-style herb seasoned stuffing
  16 mushrooms (2-inch diameter), stems removed

Heat oven to 350°. In small bowl stir together butter, carrot, green pepper, onion and stuffing. Stuff *each* mushroom cap with *1 tablespoon* filling. Place in buttered 13×9-inch baking pan. Bake for 20 to 25 minutes or until mushrooms are tender. *Makes 16 appetizers*

HERBED CHICKEN NUGGETS

*As an appetizer, snack or light meal, these herbed nuggets are sure
to be a popular menu addition.*

1¼ cups corn flake crumbs
1½ teaspoons dried oregano leaves
1½ teaspoons dried thyme leaves
1½ teaspoons ground cumin
  2 whole chicken breasts, skinned,
    boned, cut into 1-inch pieces
½ cup LAND O LAKES® Butter,
  melted

1 carton (8 ounces) dairy sour
  cream (1 cup)
2 tablespoons Dijon-style
  mustard
1 tablespoon milk

Heat oven to 425°. In small bowl stir together corn flake crumbs, oregano, thyme and cumin. Dip chicken pieces into melted butter; coat with crumb mixture. Place ½ inch apart on 15×10×1-inch ungreased jelly roll pan. Bake for 10 to 15 minutes or until fork tender and crisp. Meanwhile, in small bowl stir together sour cream, mustard and milk. Serve nuggets with mustard sauce. *Makes 50 to 60 nuggets*

Tip: Nuggets can be baked ahead of time and reheated at 350° for 10 minutes.

ITALIAN PARMESAN TWISTS

*Snacking takes a new "twist" when Italian-seasoned bread sticks are
dipped in pizza sauce.*

1 cup grated Parmesan cheese
1½ teaspoons Italian herb
  seasoning*
1 loaf frozen bread dough,
  thawed

⅓ cup LAND O LAKES® Butter,
  melted
Pizza sauce, warmed

Heat oven to 450°. In 9-inch pie pan combine Parmesan cheese and Italian seasoning. Divide dough into 8 sections; divide *each* section into 4 pieces. (There should be 32 pieces of dough.) Roll *each* piece into 4-inch rope. Dip *each* rope in melted butter; roll in Parmesan mixture. Twist rope 3 times. Place on greased cookie sheets. Bake for 7 to 9 minutes or until golden brown. Serve warm with pizza sauce. *Makes 32 twists*

*You may substitute ¼ teaspoon *each* dried oregano leaves, dried marjoram leaves and dried basil leaves and ⅛ teaspoon rubbed sage for the 1½ teaspoons Italian herb seasoning.

BUTTER CRUSTED PAN PIZZA

Serve this pan pizza plain or add sautéed peppers, shrimp or your favorite topping.

PIZZA DOUGH

1 package (¼ ounce) active dry yeast

½ cup warm water (105° to 115°F)

½ cup LAND O LAKES® Butter, melted, cooled (105° to 115°F)

3 to 3½ cups all-purpose flour

¼ cup freshly grated Parmesan cheese

2 teaspoons salt

3 eggs

TOPPING

¼ cup LAND O LAKES® Butter

3 cups (3 medium) thinly sliced onions

1 teaspoon minced fresh garlic

8 medium Roma (Italian) tomatoes, sliced ⅛ inch thick

1 teaspoon dried basil leaves

½ teaspoon coarsely ground pepper

½ cup freshly grated Parmesan cheese

For pizza dough, in large mixer bowl dissolve yeast in warm water. Add ½ cup cooled butter, *2 cups* flour, ¼ cup Parmesan cheese, salt and eggs. Beat at medium speed, scraping bowl often, until smooth, 1 to 2 minutes. By hand, stir in enough remaining flour to make dough easy to handle. Turn dough onto lightly floured surface; knead until smooth and elastic, 3 to 5 minutes. Place in greased bowl; turn greased side up. Cover; let rise in warm place until double in size about 1 hour. Dough is ready if indentation remains when touched. Punch down dough; divide in half. Let stand 10 minutes.

Heat oven to 400°. For topping, in 10-inch skillet melt ¼ cup butter until sizzling. Add onions and garlic; cook over medium heat, stirring occasionally, until onions are tender, 6 to 8 minutes. Set aside. Pat one half of dough on bottom of greased 12-inch pizza pan. Repeat for second pizza. Divide sautéed onions between pizzas. On *each* pizza arrange half of tomato slices; sprinkle *each* with *½ teaspoon* basil leaves and *¼ teaspoon* coarsely ground pepper. Sprinkle *each* with *¼ cup* Parmesan cheese. If desired, arrange additional suggested topping ingredients on pizzas. Bake for 16 to 22 minutes or until golden brown. *Makes 2 (12-inch) pizzas*

Tip: Additional suggested toppings: sautéed red, yellow *or* green peppers; tiny cooked shrimp; chopped marinated artichokes; sliced green *or* ripe olives; etc.

Butter Crusted Pan Pizza

HOMEMADE SHRIMP BUTTER

This creamy shrimp spread makes a quick and easy appetizer.

½ cup LAND O LAKES® Butter, softened
¼ cup mayonnaise
1 package (8 ounces) cream cheese, softened
3 tablespoons finely chopped onion

1 can (4¼ ounces) broken shrimp, rinsed, drained
1 tablespoon lemon juice
Assorted crackers

In small mixer bowl combine butter, mayonnaise and cream cheese. Beat at medium speed, scraping bowl often, until light and fluffy, 2 to 3 minutes. Add onion, shrimp and lemon juice; continue beating until well mixed, 1 to 2 minutes. Serve with crackers. Store refrigerated. *Makes 2 cups*

BAKED ARTICHOKE & CHEESE DIP

Dip some pieces of crusty French bread into this bubbling hot dip.

¼ cup LAND O LAKES® Butter
1 cup coarsely chopped onion (1 medium)
1 cup coarsely chopped red pepper (1 medium)
1 teaspoon minced fresh garlic
3 tablespoons all-purpose flour
1½ cups milk
2 cups (8 ounces) shredded mozzarella cheese
½ cup freshly grated Parmesan cheese

1 package (3 ounces) cream cheese, softened
½ cup chopped fresh parsley
⅓ cup mayonnaise
¼ cup lemon juice
1 can (14 ounces) artichoke hearts, drained, cut into ½-inch pieces
½ teaspoon coarsely ground pepper
1 teaspoon grated lemon peel
French bread *or* crackers

Heat oven to 375°. In 10-inch skillet melt *1 tablespoon* butter until sizzling; stir in onion, red pepper and garlic. Cook over medium heat, stirring occasionally, until vegetables are crisply tender, 1 to 2 minutes. In 2-quart saucepan melt remaining 3 tablespoons butter; stir in flour. Cook over medium heat, stirring constantly, until smooth and bubbly, 30 seconds. Stir in milk. Continue cooking, stirring occasionally, until mixture comes to a full boil, 2 to 3 minutes. Boil 1 minute. Remove from heat. Stir in mozzarella cheese, Parmesan cheese and cream cheese until melted. Stir in ¼ *cup* parsley, mayonnaise, lemon juice, artichoke hearts, pepper and lemon peel. Stir cheese mixture into sautéed vegetables. Pour into shallow 1½-quart ovenproof casserole. Bake for 25 to 30 minutes or until bubbly. Sprinkle with remaining ¼ cup parsley. Serve with French bread or crackers. *Makes 16 servings*

COUNTRY PÂTÉ

This rich pâté can make everyday crackers and slices of crisp apples special.

4 cups water
2 stalks celery, cut into 1-inch pieces
3 sprigs fresh parsley
10 peppercorns
1 pound chicken livers
1 cup LAND O LAKES® Butter, softened
1 cup (1 medium) coarsely chopped onion
2 teaspoons dry mustard
½ teaspoon ground nutmeg
¼ teaspoon ground cloves
¼ teaspoon salt
1 tablespoon brandy *or* apple juice
1 teaspoon minced fresh garlic
½ teaspoon hot pepper sauce
¼ cup chopped fresh parsley
Assorted crackers
Red and green apples and pears

In 3-quart saucepan combine water, celery, parsley sprigs and peppercorns. Cook over medium-high heat until water comes to a full boil, 3 to 5 minutes. Reduce heat to medium; add chicken livers. Continue cooking, stirring occasionally, until chicken livers are fork tender, 15 to 20 minutes. Drain; discard liquid, *reserving cooked parsley and livers.*

In food processor container place cooked parsley, livers, butter, onion, mustard, nutmeg, cloves, salt, brandy, garlic and hot pepper sauce. Blend on high speed until smooth, 1 to 2 minutes. By hand, stir in *2 tablespoons* chopped parsley. Place in serving bowl; sprinkle with remaining 2 tablespoons chopped parsley. Refrigerate at least 4 hours. Serve with crackers, apples and pears.

Makes 3 cups

Tip: Pâté can be refrigerated for 1 to 2 days. Before serving, let stand at room temperature 1 hour.

HOT BUTTERED RUM

Treat family and friends to this hot, buttery drink.

1 cup granulated sugar
1 cup firmly packed brown sugar
1 cup LAND O LAKES® Butter
2 cups vanilla ice cream, softened
Rum *or* rum extract
Boiling water
Ground nutmeg

In 2-quart saucepan combine granulated sugar, brown sugar and butter. Cook over low heat, stirring occasionally, until butter is melted and sugar is dissolved, 6 to 8 minutes. In large mixer bowl combine cooked mixture with ice cream; beat at medium speed, scraping bowl often, until smooth, 1 to 2 minutes. Store refrigerated up to 2 weeks.

For *each* serving, fill mug with *¼ cup* mixture, *1 ounce* rum or *¼ teaspoon* rum extract and *¾ cup* boiling water; sprinkle with nutmeg.

Makes 16 servings (4 cups)

Tip: Mixture can be frozen up to 1 month.

GARLIC SPINACH TURNOVERS

*Serve these spinach and red pepper turnovers as an appetizer
or with soup and salad for a simple supper.*

PASTRY
1½ cups all-purpose flour
¼ teaspoon salt
½ cup LAND O LAKES® Butter

1 egg, slightly beaten
3 tablespoons milk

FILLING
**1 tablespoon LAND O LAKES®
  Butter**
½ teaspoon minced fresh garlic
2 cups torn fresh spinach leaves
**1 cup fresh mushroom slices
  (¼ inch)**
**½ cup coarsely chopped red
  pepper (1 medium)**
**½ cup coarsely chopped onion
  (1 medium)**

**2 tablespoons freshly grated
  Parmesan cheese**
**¼ teaspoon coarsely ground
  pepper**
⅛ teaspoon salt
Dash ground red pepper
1 egg, slightly beaten
1 tablespoon milk

Heat oven to 400°. For pastry, in medium bowl combine flour and ¼ teaspoon salt; cut in ½ cup butter until crumbly. In small bowl stir together 1 egg and 3 tablespoons milk. Add egg mixture to flour mixture; stir until dough leaves side of bowl. Shape into ball. Wrap in plastic wrap; refrigerate while preparing filling.

For filling, in 10-inch skillet cook 1 tablespoon butter until sizzling; stir in garlic. Cook over medium heat, stirring occasionally, until garlic is tender, 1 to 2 minutes. Add spinach leaves, mushrooms, chopped red pepper and onion. Continue cooking, stirring occasionally, until vegetables are tender crisp, 3 to 4 minutes. Stir in Parmesan cheese, pepper, ⅛ teaspoon salt and ground red pepper. Set aside. Cut pastry dough in half.

On lightly floured surface, roll out half of dough to 12×9-inch rectangle. Cut *each* rectangle into 12 (3-inch) squares. Place *about 1 teaspoon* filling on one half of *each* square; fold other half over, forming triangle. Press edges with fork to seal. Place on ungreased cookie sheets; with knife cut 2 diagonal slits in *each* turnover. Repeat with remaining pastry dough and filling. In small bowl stir together 1 egg and 1 tablespoon milk; brush over turnovers. Bake for 8 to 12 minutes or until lightly browned.   *Makes 2 dozen turnovers*

Garlic Spinach Turnovers

BREADS

BANANA MACADAMIA NUT BREAD

Bake this flavorful banana bread and serve for breakfasts, coffees or teas.

2 cups all-purpose flour
¾ cup sugar
½ cup LAND O LAKES® Butter,
   softened
2 eggs
1 teaspoon baking soda
½ teaspoon salt
1 tablespoon grated orange peel

1 teaspoon vanilla
1 cup mashed ripe bananas
   (2 medium)
¼ cup orange juice
1 cup flaked coconut
1 jar (3½ ounces) coarsely
   chopped macadamia nuts *or*
   walnuts (¾ cup)

Heat oven to 350°. In large mixer bowl combine flour, sugar, butter, eggs, baking soda, salt, orange peel and vanilla. Beat at low speed, scraping bowl often, until well mixed, 2 to 3 minutes. Add bananas and orange juice. Continue beating, scraping bowl often, until well mixed, 1 minute. By hand, stir in coconut and nuts. (Batter will be thick.) Spread into 1 greased 9×5-inch loaf pan or 3 greased 5½×3-inch mini-loaf pans.

Bake 9×5-inch loaf for 60 to 65 minutes or mini loaves for 35 to 45 minutes, or until wooden pick inserted in center comes out clean. Cool 10 minutes; remove from pans. *Makes 1 (9×5-inch) loaf or 3 mini loaves*

Banana Macadamia Nut Bread

MINI ALMOND PASTRIES

These mini pastries have a sweet almond flavor.

¼ cup powdered sugar
¼ cup LAND O LAKES® Butter, softened
1 tube (3½ ounces) almond paste (⅓ cup)
2 egg yolks

2 teaspoons grated lemon peel
½ teaspoon almond extract
¼ cup granulated sugar
1 package (17¼ ounces) frozen prerolled sheets puff pastry, thawed (2 sheets)

In small mixer bowl combine powdered sugar, butter, almond paste, egg yolks, lemon peel and almond extract. Beat at low speed, scraping bowl often, until well mixed, 1 to 2 minutes; set aside. Sprinkle about *1 tablespoon* granulated sugar on surface or pastry cloth. Unfold 1 sheet puff pastry on sugared surface; sprinkle with about *1 tablespoon* granulated sugar. Roll out puff pastry sheet into 12-inch square. Cut square into 2 (12×6-inch) rectangles. Spread ¼ of (*about 3 tablespoons*) almond paste mixture on *each* rectangle. Working with 1 (12×6-inch) rectangle at a time, fold ½ inch of both 12-inch sides in toward center of pastry. Continue folding both 12-inch sides, ½ inch at a time, until 12-inch sides meet in center. Fold one 12-inch side on top of other 12-inch side; firmly press layers together. Repeat with remaining 12×6-inch rectangle. Repeat with remaining ingredients. Wrap *each* pastry roll in plastic wrap; refrigerate at least 2 hours.

Heat oven to 400°. Cut pastry rolls into ½-inch slices. Place slices 2 inches apart on greased or parchment-lined cookie sheets. Bake for 7 to 11 minutes or until lightly browned. Remove from pan immediately.

Makes 7 to 8 dozen pastries

CURRANT BISCUITS

Serve these cutout biscuits warm, with shaved ham and honey mustard, for a festive breakfast or brunch.

2 cups all-purpose flour
2 tablespoons sugar
2 teaspoons baking powder
½ teaspoon ground ginger
¼ teaspoon ground nutmeg
¼ teaspoon salt
1 teaspoon grated orange peel

½ cup LAND O LAKES® Butter
¼ cup shortening
½ cup half-and-half
½ cup currants *or* raisins
2 tablespoons LAND O LAKES® Butter, melted

Heat oven to 400°. In large bowl combine flour, sugar, baking powder, ginger, nutmeg, salt and orange peel. Cut in ½ cup butter and shortening until crumbly. Stir in half-and-half and currants just until moistened. Turn out dough onto lightly floured surface; knead until smooth, 1 minute. Roll out dough to ¾-inch thickness. With 3-inch star or favorite cutter, cut out 8 to 10 biscuits. Place 1 inch apart on ungreased cookie sheet. Brush tops with some of the melted butter. Bake for 10 to 12 minutes or until lightly browned. Brush tops with remaining melted butter.

Makes 8 to 10 biscuits

Mini Almond Pastries

"Sugarplum" wreath

CINNAMON & PECAN COFFEE CAKE

This pull-apart yeast bread makes a great breakfast treat.

1 cup milk
¼ cup LAND O LAKES® Butter
1 package (¼ ounce) active dry
   yeast
¼ cup warm water (105° to 115°F)
3½ to 3¾ cups all-purpose flour
1¼ cups sugar

1 egg
1 teaspoon salt
½ cup chopped pecans
1½ teaspoons ground cinnamon
½ cup LAND O LAKES® Butter,
   melted
½ cup golden raisins

In 1-quart saucepan heat milk until it just comes to a boil, 3 to 4 minutes; stir in ¼ cup butter until melted. Cool to lukewarm (105° to 115°F). In large mixer bowl dissolve yeast in warm water. Add cooled milk mixture, *2 cups* flour, *¼ cup* sugar, egg and salt. Beat at medium speed, scraping bowl often, until smooth, 1 to 2 minutes. Stir in enough remaining flour to make dough easy to handle. Turn dough onto lightly floured surface; knead until smooth and elastic, about 10 minutes. Place in greased bowl; turn greased side up. Cover; let rise in warm place until double in size, about 1½ hours. Dough is ready if indentation remains when touched. Punch down dough; divide in half. With floured hands shape *each* half into 24 balls.

In small bowl stir together remaining 1 cup sugar, pecans and cinnamon. Dip balls first in melted butter, then in sugar mixture. Place 24 balls in bottom of greased 10-inch tube pan or Bundt® pan. (If removable bottom tube pan, line with aluminum foil.) Sprinkle with raisins. Top with remaining 24 balls. Cover; let rise in warm place until double in size, about 45 minutes. Heat oven to 375°. Bake for 35 to 40 minutes or until coffee cake sounds hollow when tapped. (Cover with aluminum foil if coffee cake browns too quickly.) Immediately invert pan on heat-proof serving plate. Let pan stand 1 minute to allow sugar mixture to drizzle over cake. Remove pan; serve warm.   *Makes 1 coffee cake*

CHOCOLATE CHIP SCONES

Traditional scones with a new twist.

1¾ cups all-purpose flour
3 tablespoons sugar
2½ teaspoons baking powder
½ teaspoon salt
⅓ cup LAND O LAKES® Butter

1 egg, slightly beaten
½ cup semi-sweet chocolate chips
4 to 6 tablespoons half-and-half
1 egg, slightly beaten

Heat oven to 400°. In medium bowl combine flour, sugar, baking powder and salt. Cut butter into flour mixture until it resembles fine crumbs. Stir in 1 egg, chocolate chips and just enough half-and-half so dough leaves side of bowl. Turn dough onto lightly floured surface; knead lightly 10 times. Roll into ½-inch-thick circle; cut into 12 wedges. Place on ungreased cookie sheet. Brush with remaining egg. Bake for 10 to 12 minutes or until golden brown. Immediately remove from cookie sheet. Serve warm.   *Makes 1 dozen scones*

Cinnamon & Pecan Coffee Cake

LEMON BUTTER CRESCENT ROLLS

Melt-in-your-mouth buttery dinner rolls with two unique flavorful fillings.

CRESCENT ROLLS

⅓ cup sugar
½ cup LAND O LAKES® Butter
½ cup milk
¾ teaspoon salt
1 package (¼ ounce) active dry
    yeast
½ cup warm water (105° to 115°F)

1 egg
1 tablespoon grated lemon peel
3½ to 4 cups all-purpose flour
¼ cup LAND O LAKES® Butter,
    softened
1 egg, slightly beaten
1 tablespoon milk

FILLING VARIATIONS

Lemon Anise
   1 teaspoon anise seed
   2 teaspoons grated lemon peel

Walnut Thyme
   1 cup coarsely chopped walnuts
   1 teaspoon chopped fresh thyme
      leaves*

For crescent rolls, in 1-quart saucepan combine sugar, ½ cup butter, ½ cup milk and salt. Cook over medium heat, stirring occasionally, until butter is melted, 4 to 5 minutes. Cool to warm (105° to 115°F). In large mixer bowl dissolve yeast in warm water; add butter mixture, 1 egg, 1 tablespoon lemon peel and *2 cups* flour. Beat at medium speed, scraping bowl often, until smooth, 1 to 2 minutes. By hand, stir in enough remaining flour to make dough easy to handle. Turn dough onto lightly floured surface; knead until smooth and elastic, 5 to 6 minutes. Place in greased bowl; turn greased side up. Cover; let rise in warm place until double in size, about 1½ hours. Dough is ready if indentation remains when touched. Punch down dough; divide in half. Let stand 10 minutes.

On lightly floured surface roll *half* of dough into 12-inch circle. Spread with 2 *tablespoons* softened butter. If desired, sprinkle with *half* of anise seed and lemon peel or *half* of walnuts and thyme. Cut circle of dough into 12 wedges. Roll *each* wedge into crescent shape. Place on greased cookie sheets. Repeat with remaining half of dough. Cover; let rise in warm place 15 minutes.

Heat oven to 375°. Bake for 10 to 12 minutes or until lightly browned. Meanwhile, in small bowl stir together beaten egg and 1 tablespoon milk. Brush on rolls. Continue baking for 2 to 3 minutes or until golden brown.

Makes 2 dozen rolls

*You may substitute ½ teaspoon dried thyme leaves for the 1 teaspoon chopped fresh thyme leaves.

FRESH SAGE & PEPPER POPOVERS

Serve these tender seasoned popovers with sage butter.

POPOVERS

3 eggs, room temperature
1¼ cups milk, room temperature
1¼ cups all-purpose flour
1½ teaspoons fresh sage leaves,*
  rubbed

¼ teaspoon coarsely ground
  pepper
¼ teaspoon salt

SAGE BUTTER

½ cup LAND O LAKES® Butter,
  softened
1½ teaspoons fresh sage leaves,*
  rubbed

¼ teaspoon coarsely ground
  pepper

Heat oven to 450°. For popovers, in small mixer bowl beat eggs at medium speed, scraping bowl often, until light yellow, 1 to 2 minutes. Add milk; continue beating for 1 minute to incorporate air. By hand, stir in all remaining popover ingredients. Pour batter into greased 6 cup popover pan or 6 custard cups. Bake for 15 minutes; *reduce temperature to 350°. Do not open oven.* Continue baking for 25 to 30 minutes or until golden brown.

For Sage Butter, in small mixer bowl beat all Sage Butter ingredients at low speed, scraping bowl often, until light and fluffy, 1 to 2 minutes; set aside.

Insert knife in popovers to allow steam to escape. Serve immediately with Sage Butter. *Makes 6 popovers*

Tip: Eggs and milk should be at room temperature (72°F) to help ensure successful popovers.

*You may substitute ½ teaspoon dried sage leaves, crumbled, for the 1½ teaspoons fresh sage leaves, rubbed.

GLAZED TRIPLE CHOCOLATE BREAD

This chocolate cake-like bread, studded with chocolate chips and frosted with more chocolate, makes a great homemade gift.

BREAD
- ⅔ cup firmly packed brown sugar
- ½ cup LAND O LAKES® Butter, softened
- 1 cup semi-sweet miniature real chocolate chips, melted
- 2 eggs
- 2½ cups all-purpose flour
- 1½ cups applesauce
- 1 teaspoon baking powder
- 1 teaspoon baking soda
- 2 teaspoons vanilla
- ½ cup semi-sweet miniature real chocolate chips

GLAZE
- ½ cup semi-sweet miniature real chocolate chips
- 1 tablespoon LAND O LAKES® Butter
- 5 teaspoons water
- ½ cup powdered sugar
- ¼ teaspoon vanilla
- Dash salt

Heat oven to 350°. For bread, in large mixer bowl combine brown sugar and ½ cup butter. Beat at medium speed, scraping bowl often, until creamy, 1 to 2 minutes. Add 1 cup melted chocolate chips and eggs; continue beating until well mixed, 1 to 2 minutes. Add flour, applesauce, baking powder, baking soda and 2 teaspoons vanilla. Reduce speed to low; continue beating, scraping bowl often, until creamy, 1 to 2 minutes. By hand, stir in ½ cup chocolate chips. Spoon batter into 5 greased 5½×3-inch mini-loaf pans. Bake for 35 to 42 minutes or until center crack is dry when touched. Cool 10 minutes. Remove from pans. (Bread can be frozen unglazed. Remove from freezer; bring to room temperature before glazing.)

For glaze, in 2-quart saucepan combine ½ cup chocolate chips, 1 tablespoon butter and water. Cook over low heat, stirring constantly, until melted and smooth. Remove from heat. Stir in powdered sugar, ¼ teaspoon vanilla and salt until smooth and creamy. Drizzle *each* warm loaf with glaze. Cool completely. *Makes 5 mini loaves*

Glazed Triple Chocolate Bread

SPARKLING CRANBERRY MUFFINS

The butter and sugar coating is what makes these homemade muffins special.

1 cup chopped fresh cranberries
2 tablespoons sugar
2 cups all-purpose flour
⅓ cup sugar
2 teaspoons baking powder
½ teaspoon salt

½ cup LAND O LAKES® Butter
¾ cup orange juice
1 egg, slightly beaten
¼ cup LAND O LAKES® Butter, melted
¼ cup sugar

Heat oven to 400°. In small bowl combine cranberries and 2 tablespoons sugar; set aside. In large bowl stir together flour, ⅓ cup sugar, baking powder and salt. Cut in ½ cup butter until mixture is crumbly. Stir in orange juice and egg just until moistened. Fold in cranberry-sugar mixture. Spoon batter into greased 12-cup muffin pan. Bake for 20 to 25 minutes or until golden brown. Cool 5 minutes; remove from pan. Dip top of *each* muffin in ¼ cup melted butter, then in ¼ cup sugar. Serve warm.   *Makes 1 dozen muffins*

LEMON POPPY SEED BREAD

Everyone will enjoy these mini loaves of lemon glazed bread.

BREAD
2¼ cups all-purpose flour
1¼ cups sugar
¾ cup milk
1 cup LAND O LAKES® Butter, softened

3 eggs
2 tablespoons poppy seed
1½ teaspoons baking powder
1 teaspoon salt
1 tablespoon grated lemon peel

GLAZE
⅓ cup sugar
3 tablespoons LAND O LAKES® Butter, melted

1½ tablespoons lemon juice

Heat oven to 350°. For bread, grease bottom only of 4 (5½×3-inch) mini-loaf pans. In large mixer bowl combine all bread ingredients. Beat at medium speed, scraping bowl often, until well mixed, 2 to 3 minutes. Pour into prepared pans. Bake for 30 to 40 minutes or until wooden pick inserted in center comes out clean.

For glaze, in small bowl stir together all glaze ingredients. Pour over warm bread loaves. Cool 10 minutes. Loosen edge of loaves with knife; remove from pans.   *Makes 4 mini loaves*

Sparkling Cranberry Muffins

ONION FENNEL BREAD STICKS

Serve these flavorful bread sticks tied in a festive napkin.

1 tablespoon fennel seed
¼ cup LAND O LAKES® Butter
1 cup finely chopped onion
   (1 medium)
1 package (¼ ounce) active dry
   yeast
1¼ cups warm water (105° to 115°F)

1 tablespoon sugar
1 teaspoon salt
2¾ to 3¼ cups all-purpose flour
Water
Coarse salt
Coarsely ground pepper

In 10-inch skillet cook fennel seed over medium heat until toasted, 3 to 4 minutes; set aside. In same skillet melt butter until sizzling; add onion. Cook over medium heat, stirring occasionally, until onion is tender, 8 to 10 minutes. Cool to lukewarm. Meanwhile, in large bowl dissolve yeast in 1¼ cups water; stir in sugar. Let stand 5 minutes. Stir in 1 teaspoon salt and *1 cup* flour until smooth. Add onion mixture, fennel seed and enough remaining flour to form soft dough. Turn dough onto lightly floured surface; knead until smooth and elastic, 4 to 5 minutes. (Dough will be soft and slightly sticky.) Place in greased bowl; turn greased side up. Cover; let rise in warm place until double in size, about 1 hour. Dough is ready if indentation remains when touched. Punch down dough; divide in half. Let stand 10 minutes.

Heat oven to 400°. Meanwhile, divide *each* half of dough into 12 equal pieces. With lightly floured hands, on lightly floured surface form *each* piece of dough into 12-inch rope. Place on greased cookie sheets. Brush *each* bread stick with water; sprinkle with coarse salt and pepper. Bake for 12 to 16 minutes or until lightly browned. Serve warm. *Makes 2 dozen bread sticks*

MOCHA CREAM PUFF COFFEE CAKE

This delicious coffee cake features a pastry bottom, a cream puff-like center and a coffee-flavored glaze, finished with a drizzle of chocolate.

PASTRY
½ cup LAND O LAKES® Butter
1 cup all-purpose flour
2 tablespoons water

¼ cup semi-sweet miniature real chocolate chips

TOPPING
1 cup water
½ cup LAND O LAKES® Butter
1 cup all-purpose flour

1 teaspoon vanilla
3 eggs

GLAZE
1 teaspoon instant coffee granules
2 tablespoons warm water
1½ cups powdered sugar
2 tablespoons LAND O LAKES® Butter, softened

¼ cup semi-sweet miniature real chocolate chips
1 teaspoon vegetable oil

Heat oven to 350°. For pastry, in large bowl cut ½ cup butter into 1 cup flour until crumbly. With fork mix in 2 tablespoons water. Gather pastry into a ball; divide into 2 equal portions. On ungreased cookie sheet pat *each* portion into 12×3-inch rectangle about 3 inches apart. Sprinkle 2 *tablespoons* chocolate chips over *each* half; press gently.

For topping, in 2-quart saucepan combine 1 cup water and ½ cup butter. Cook over medium heat until mixture comes to a full boil, 6 to 8 minutes. Remove from heat; stir in 1 cup flour and vanilla. Cook over low heat, stirring constantly, until mixture forms a ball, about 1 minute. Remove from heat. By hand, beat in eggs, 1 at a time, until smooth and glossy. Spread *half* of egg mixture over *each* rectangle. (Chocolate chips may melt and swirl into egg mixture.)

Bake for 55 to 65 minutes or until surface is crisp and golden brown; cool completely. (Topping rises during baking and shrinks during standing forming a custard-like layer.)

For glaze, in small bowl dissolve coffee in 2 tablespoons warm water; stir in powdered sugar and 2 tablespoons butter until smooth and creamy. Spread *each* cooled coffee cake with about ¼ cup glaze. In 1-quart saucepan combine ¼ cup chocolate chips and vegetable oil. Cook over medium-low heat, stirring constantly, until chocolate is melted, 2 to 4 minutes. Drizzle *half* of mixture over *each* coffee cake. Cut *each* coffee cake into 1-inch slices.

Makes 2 coffee cakes

COOKIES

CHOCOLATE-DIPPED CRESCENTS

These easy-to-make crescent cookies taste even better when dipped into melted chocolate.

1½ cups powdered sugar
1 cup LAND O LAKES® Butter, softened
1 egg
1½ teaspoons almond extract
2½ cups all-purpose flour

1 teaspoon cream of tartar
1 teaspoon baking soda
1 package (6 ounces) semi-sweet real chocolate chips (1 cup), melted
Powdered sugar

Heat oven to 375°. In large mixer bowl combine 1½ cups powdered sugar and butter. Beat at medium speed, scraping bowl often, until creamy, 1 to 2 minutes. Add egg and almond extract; continue beating until well mixed, 1 to 2 minutes. Reduce speed to low. Add flour, cream of tartar and baking soda. Continue beating, scraping bowl often, until well mixed, 1 to 2 minutes. Shape into 1-inch balls. Roll balls into 2-inch ropes; shape into crescents. Place 2 inches apart on ungreased cookie sheets. Bake for 8 to 10 minutes or until set. Cookies do not brown. Cool completely. Dip half of *each* cookie into chocolate; sprinkle remaining half with powdered sugar. Refrigerate until set.

Makes about 4½ dozen cookies

Chocolate-Dipped Crescents

"Marilyn's snowdrops" CHOCOLATE PIXIES

*These chocolate cookies' powdered sugar coating forms a
unique crinkled design during baking.*

¼ cup LAND O LAKES® Butter
4 squares (1 ounce *each*)
  unsweetened chocolate
2 cups all-purpose flour
2 cups granulated sugar

4 eggs
2 teaspoons baking powder
½ teaspoon salt
½ cup chopped walnuts *or* pecans
  Powdered sugar

In 1-quart saucepan melt butter and chocolate over low heat, 8 to 10 minutes; cool. In large mixer bowl combine melted chocolate mixture, *1 cup* flour, granulated sugar, eggs, baking powder and salt. Beat at medium speed, scraping bowl often, until well mixed, 2 to 3 minutes. By hand, stir in remaining 1 cup flour and walnuts. Cover; refrigerate until firm, 2 hours or overnight.

Heat oven to 300°. Shape rounded teaspoonfuls of dough into 1-inch balls; roll in powdered sugar. Place 2 inches apart on greased cookie sheets. Bake for 12 to 15 minutes or until firm to the touch. Remove immediately. Cool completely. *Makes about 4 dozen cookies*

LEMON-BUTTER SNOWBARS

These classic, buttery lemon bars are an all-time favorite.

CRUST
1⅓ cups all-purpose flour
 ¼ cup granulated sugar

½ cup LAND O LAKES® Butter,
  softened

FILLING
 ¾ cup granulated sugar
 2 eggs
 2 tablespoons all-purpose flour

¼ teaspoon baking powder
3 tablespoons lemon juice
  Powdered sugar

Heat oven to 350°. For crust, in small mixer bowl combine all crust ingredients. Beat at low speed, scraping bowl often, until mixture is crumbly, 2 to 3 minutes. Press on bottom of ungreased 8-inch square baking pan. Bake for 15 to 20 minutes or until edges are lightly browned.

For filling, in small mixer bowl combine all filling ingredients *except* powdered sugar. Beat at low speed, scraping bowl often, until well mixed. Pour filling over hot crust. Continue baking for 18 to 20 minutes or until filling is set. Sprinkle with powdered sugar; cool completely. Cut into bars; sprinkle again with powdered sugar. *Makes 16 bars*

*Chocolate Pixies;
Lemon-Butter Snowbars*

MAPLE-NUT COOKIES

A tender butter cookie flavored with maple and topped with a pecan.

2½ cups all-purpose flour
 ¾ cup firmly packed brown sugar
 1 cup LAND O LAKES® Butter,
   softened
 2 eggs

½ teaspoon baking powder
¼ teaspoon salt
½ teaspoon maple extract
1 package (5 ounces) pecan halves
   (about 54)

Heat oven to 400°. In large mixer bowl combine flour, brown sugar, butter, eggs, baking powder, salt and maple extract. Beat at low speed, scraping bowl often, until well mixed, 3 to 4 minutes. If dough is too soft, cover; refrigerate until firm, 30 to 60 minutes. Shape rounded teaspoonfuls of dough into 1-inch balls. Place 2 inches apart on ungreased cookie sheets. Press 1 pecan half into center of *each* cookie. Bake for 7 to 9 minutes or until edges are lightly browned. *Makes about 4½ dozen cookies*

CHOCOLATE CARAMEL OATMEAL BARS

These chewy caramel bars are sinfully delicious.

CRUMB MIXTURE
1½ cups all-purpose flour
 1 cup quick-cooking oats
 1 cup firmly packed brown sugar

¾ cup LAND O LAKES® Butter,
   softened
¾ teaspoon baking soda
½ teaspoon salt

CARAMEL MIXTURE
 ½ cup milk

1 package (14 ounces) caramels,
   unwrapped (48)

FILLING
 1 cup semi-sweet real chocolate
   chips
 ½ cup chopped pecans

1 cup semi-sweet real chocolate
   chips, melted
1 package (5 ounces) pecan halves
   (60)

Heat oven to 350°. For crumb mixture, in large mixer bowl combine all crumb mixture ingredients. Beat at medium speed, scraping bowl often, until mixture is crumbly, 2 to 3 minutes. *Reserve 1 cup crumb mixture*; set aside. Press remaining mixture on bottom of 13×9-inch baking pan. Bake for 10 minutes.

For caramel mixture, in 2-quart saucepan combine milk and caramels. Cook over medium low heat, stirring occasionally, until caramels melt and mixture is creamy, 15 to 20 minutes.

For filling, sprinkle 1 cup chocolate chips and ½ cup chopped pecans over partially baked crust. Pour caramel mixture evenly over chocolate chips and pecans. Sprinkle with reserved crumb mixture; pat lightly. Continue baking for 18 to 22 minutes or until caramel is bubbly around edges. Cool completely; cut into bars. On *each* bar, place ½ *teaspoon* melted chocolate; top with pecan half. Store in tightly covered container. *Makes 5 dozen bars*

PEANUT BUTTER CHOCOLATE BARS

These bars are "heavenly" good.

CRUST

1 cup all-purpose flour
⅓ cup sugar

½ cup LAND O LAKES® Butter,
   softened

FILLING

½ cup sugar
¼ cup crunchy-style peanut butter
½ cup light corn syrup
2 eggs

¼ teaspoon salt
½ teaspoon vanilla
½ cup flaked coconut
½ cup semi-sweet chocolate chips

Heat oven to 350°. For crust, in small mixer bowl combine all crust ingredients. Beat at low speed, scraping bowl often, until mixture is crumbly, 1 to 2 minutes. Press on bottom of greased 9-inch square baking pan. Bake for 12 to 17 minutes or until edges are lightly browned.

For filling, in same mixer bowl combine ½ cup sugar, peanut butter, corn syrup, eggs, salt and vanilla. Beat at low speed, scraping bowl often, until well mixed, 1 to 2 minutes. By hand, stir in coconut and chocolate chips; pour over crust. Return to oven; continue baking for 20 to 30 minutes or until filling is set and golden brown. Cool completely. Cut into bars.   *Makes 3 dozen bars*

RASPBERRY FILLED TARTS

Raspberry preserves fill these lemon flavored pastries.

2¾ cups all-purpose flour
1 cup LAND O LAKES® Butter,
   softened
1 carton (8 ounces) dairy sour
   cream (1 cup)

2 tablespoons grated lemon peel
1 cup raspberry preserves*
   Powdered sugar

Heat oven to 400°. In large mixer bowl combine *1 cup* flour, butter, sour cream and lemon peel. Beat at medium speed, scraping bowl often, until well mixed, 2 to 3 minutes. By hand, stir in remaining 1¾ cups flour until well mixed. On well-floured surface, roll out dough, ⅓ at a time, to 12×9-inch rectangle. With sharp knife, cut into 12 (3-inch) squares. Place squares on ungreased cookie sheets. Repeat with remaining dough. Place *about 1 teaspoon* preserves in center of *each* square. Bring together 4 corners of *each* square and pinch to hold together. Bake for 11 to 14 minutes or until lightly browned. Cool completely; sprinkle with powdered sugar.   *Makes 3 dozen cookies*

*You may substitute 1 cup of your favorite flavor preserves for the 1 cup raspberry preserves.

FUDGY ROCKY ROAD BROWNIES

These rich brownies, topped with crunchy peanuts and creamy marshmallows, will disappear fast.

BROWNIES

1 cup LAND O LAKES® Butter
4 squares (1 ounce *each*)
 unsweetened chocolate
2 cups granulated sugar

1½ cups all-purpose flour
4 eggs
2 teaspoons vanilla
½ cup chopped salted peanuts

FROSTING

¼ cup LAND O LAKES® Butter
1 package (3 ounces) cream cheese
1 square (1 ounce) unsweetened
 chocolate
¼ cup milk

2¾ cups powdered sugar
1 teaspoon vanilla
2 cups miniature marshmallows
1 cup salted peanuts

Heat oven to 350°. For brownies, in 3-quart saucepan combine 1 cup butter and 4 squares chocolate. Cook over medium heat, stirring constantly, until melted, 5 to 7 minutes. Stir in granulated sugar, flour, eggs and 2 teaspoons vanilla until well mixed. Stir in ½ cup chopped peanuts. Spread into greased 13×9-inch baking pan. Bake for 20 to 25 minutes or until brownies start to pull away from sides of pan.

For frosting, in 2-quart saucepan combine ¼ cup butter, cream cheese, 1 square chocolate and milk. Cook over medium heat, stirring occasionally, until melted, 6 to 8 minutes. Remove from heat; stir in powdered sugar and 1 teaspoon vanilla until smooth. Stir in marshmallows and 1 cup peanuts. Immediately spread over hot brownies. Cool completely; cut into bars. Store refrigerated.

Makes 4 dozen bars

CHEWY CANDY CRUNCH BARS

A chewy caramel coats crisp cereal in this sure-to-please bar.

4 cups bite-size crispy corn cereal
 squares
1 cup salted peanuts
1 package (8 ounces) candy coated
 milk chocolate pieces (1 cup)

½ cup LAND O LAKES® Butter
1 cup firmly packed brown sugar
½ cup light corn syrup
2 tablespoons all-purpose flour

In large bowl combine cereal, peanuts and candies; set aside. In 2-quart saucepan melt butter, 2 to 4 minutes. Stir in all remaining ingredients. Cook over medium heat, stirring occasionally, until mixture comes to a full boil, 2 to 4 minutes. Boil 1 minute. Pour caramel mixture over cereal mixture; toss to coat well. Press on bottom of greased 13×9-inch pan. Cool completely; cut into bars.

Makes 2 dozen bars

Fudgy Rocky Road Brownies

CHERRY DATE SKILLET COOKIES

Snowy coconut coats these made-in-the-skillet, buttery date cookies.

1 cup LAND O LAKES® Butter
1 cup firmly packed brown sugar
1 package (8 ounces) chopped
  dates
1 egg
3 cups crisp rice cereal

1 cup flaked coconut
½ cup chopped maraschino
  cherries, drained
1 tablespoon vanilla
2½ cups flaked coconut

In 10-inch skillet melt butter over medium heat. Stir in brown sugar and dates; remove from heat. Stir in egg; return to heat. Cook over medium heat, stirring constantly, until mixture comes to a full boil, 4 to 6 minutes. Boil, stirring constantly, 1 minute; remove from heat. Stir in rice cereal, 1 cup flaked coconut, cherries and vanilla until moistened. Let stand 10 minutes. Shape rounded teaspoonfuls of dough into 1-inch balls. Roll in 2½ cups coconut.

Makes about 5 dozen cookies

PECAN TARTLETS

Bite-size shortbread tarts filled with caramel and pecans.

TART SHELLS
½ cup LAND O LAKES® Butter,
  softened
½ cup granulated sugar
1 egg

1 teaspoon almond extract
1¾ cups all-purpose flour

FILLING
1 cup powdered sugar
½ cup LAND O LAKES® Butter
⅓ cup dark corn syrup

1 cup chopped pecans
36 pecan halves

Heat oven to 400°. For tart shells, in large mixer bowl combine all tart shell ingredients. Beat at medium speed, scraping bowl often, until mixture is crumbly, 2 to 3 minutes. Press 1 tablespoon mixture into cups of mini-muffin pans to form 36 (1¾- to 2-inch) shells. Bake for 7 to 10 minutes or until very lightly browned. Remove from oven. *Reduce oven to 350°.*

For filling, in 2-quart saucepan combine powdered sugar, ½ cup butter and corn syrup. Cook over medium heat, stirring occasionally, until mixture comes to a full boil, 4 to 5 minutes. Remove from heat; stir in chopped pecans. Spoon into baked shells. Top *each* with a pecan half. Bake for 5 minutes. Cool completely; remove from pans.

Makes 3 dozen tartlets

Cherry Date Skillet Cookies

APRICOT OATMEAL BARS

These quick and easy bars blend tangy apricot and chewy oatmeal for a naturally good treat.

CRUMB MIXTURE

1¼ cups all-purpose flour
1¼ cups quick-cooking oats
½ cup sugar
¾ cup LAND O LAKES® Butter, melted

½ teaspoon baking soda
¼ teaspoon salt
2 teaspoons vanilla

FILLING

1 jar (10 ounces) apricot preserves   ½ cup flaked coconut

Heat oven to 350°. For crumb mixture, in large mixer bowl combine all crumb mixture ingredients. Beat at low speed, scraping bowl often, until mixture is crumbly, 1 to 2 minutes. *Reserve 1 cup crumb mixture;* press remaining crumb mixture on bottom of greased 13×9-inch baking pan.

For filling, spread apricot preserves to within ½ inch from edge of crumb mixture; sprinkle with reserved crumb mixture and coconut. Bake for 22 to 27 minutes or until edges are lightly browned. Cool completely. Cut into bars.

Makes 3 dozen bars

OLD-WORLD RASPBERRY BARS

This buttery good raspberry-filled bar combines the goodness of Old-World baking and updated convenience.

CRUMB MIXTURE

2¼ cups all-purpose flour
1 cup sugar
1 cup chopped pecans

1 cup LAND O LAKES® Butter, softened
1 egg

FILLING

1 jar (10 ounces) raspberry preserves

Heat oven to 350°. For crumb mixture, in large mixer bowl combine all crumb mixture ingredients. Beat at low speed, scraping bowl often, until mixture is crumbly, 2 to 3 minutes. *Reserve 1½ cups crumb mixture;* press remaining crumb mixture on bottom of greased 8-inch square baking pan. Spread preserves to within ½ inch from edge of unbaked crumb mixture. Crumble remaining crumb mixture over preserves. Bake for 42 to 50 minutes or until lightly browned. Cool completely. Cut into bars.

Makes 2 dozen bars

Apricot Oatmeal Bars;
Old-World Raspberry Bars

CHEERY CHERRY MACAROONS

Satisfying and elegant, this macaroon-type cookie is filled with cherries and nuts.

3 cups all-purpose flour
1 cup sugar
1 cup LAND O LAKES® Butter,
    softened
¼ cup milk
1 egg
1 teaspoon baking powder

¼ teaspoon salt
1 teaspoon almond extract
½ cup chopped pecans
½ cup maraschino cherries,
    chopped, *well drained*
2 cups flaked coconut

Heat oven to 350°. In large mixer bowl combine flour, sugar, butter, milk, egg, baking powder, salt and almond extract. Beat at low speed, scraping bowl often, until well mixed, 2 to 3 minutes. By hand, stir in pecans and maraschino cherries. Drop rounded teaspoonfuls of dough in coconut; roll into 1-inch balls. Place 1 inch apart on ungreased cookie sheets. Bake for 15 to 20 minutes or until lightly browned (coconut will be toasted). Let stand 1 minute on cookie sheets; remove to wire rack. Cool completely. Store in tightly covered container. *Makes about 4 dozen cookies*

CITRUS SLICE 'N' BAKE COOKIES

The flavors of orange and lemon shine in these delicate butter cookies.

COOKIE

2 cups all-purpose flour
1¼ cups powdered sugar
¾ cup LAND O LAKES® Butter,
    softened
1 egg

1 teaspoon baking powder
½ teaspoon salt
¼ teaspoon baking soda
1 teaspoon grated orange peel
2 teaspoons lemon extract

SUGAR

¼ cup granulated sugar
4 drops yellow food coloring
2 drops red food coloring

2 tablespoons LAND O LAKES®
    Butter, melted

For cookies, in large mixer bowl combine all cookie ingredients. Beat at low speed, scraping bowl often, until well mixed, 2 to 3 minutes. Mold dough into 2 rolls *each* 6 inches long. Wrap in waxed paper; refrigerate at least 2 hours.

For sugar, in medium jar combine granulated sugar and yellow food coloring; cover. Shake until well blended, 1 to 2 minutes. Remove 2 tablespoons colored sugar; add red food coloring to remaining sugar. Cover; shake until well blended, 1 to 2 minutes. Heat oven to 375°. Cut *each* roll in half lengthwise; brush with 2 tablespoons melted butter. Roll 2 halves in yellow sugar and 2 halves in orange sugar. Cut rolls into ¼-inch-thick slices. Place 1 inch apart on ungreased cookie sheets. Bake for 7 to 10 minutes or until edges are lightly browned. *Makes about 4 dozen cookies*

CHOCOLATE TOFFEE BROWNIES

Toffee candy bars add extra flavor to these chewy chocolate brownies.

¼ cup LAND O LAKES® Butter
1 cup sugar
6 tablespoons unsweetened cocoa
2 eggs

¾ cup all-purpose flour
5 to 6 bars (5 to 5¼ ounces *total*)
   chocolate-coated toffee candy
   bars, chopped

Heat oven to 350°. In 2-quart saucepan melt butter. Stir in all remaining ingredients. Spread into greased 9-inch square baking pan. Bake for 20 to 25 minutes or until set. Cool completely; cut into bars.   *Makes 16 bars*

CHIPPER BARS

Chocolate chips and peanut butter make these easy-to-prepare bars everyone's favorite.

2 cups quick-cooking oats
1 cup all-purpose flour
1 cup firmly packed brown sugar
¾ cup LAND O LAKES® Butter,
   softened
½ teaspoon baking soda

½ teaspoon salt
1 can (14 ounces) sweetened
   condensed milk
⅓ cup peanut butter
1 package (6 ounces) semi-sweet
   chocolate chips (1 cup)

Heat oven to 350°. In large mixer bowl combine oats, flour, brown sugar, butter, baking soda and salt. Beat at medium speed, scraping bowl often, until crumbly, 2 to 3 minutes. *Reserve 1½ cups crumb mixture;* set aside. Press remaining crumbs on bottom of greased 13×9-inch baking pan. In small bowl stir together sweetened condensed milk and peanut butter. Pour evenly over crumb mixture in pan; sprinkle with chocolate chips. Pat reserved crumb mixture into filling. Bake for 25 to 35 minutes or until light golden brown. Cool completely; cut into bars.   *Makes 3 dozen bars*

NO-BAKE ROCKY ROAD CHOCOLATE BARS

It only takes six ingredients to make these no-bake bars.

½ cup LAND O LAKES® Butter
1 package (12 ounces) semi-sweet
   real chocolate chips (2 cups)
1 cup butterscotch chips

1 cup peanut butter
4 cups crispy rice cereal
3 cups miniature marshmallows

In Dutch oven combine butter, chocolate chips and butterscotch chips. Cook over low heat, stirring constantly, until melted, 4 to 6 minutes. Stir in peanut butter until well blended. Remove from heat. Stir in cereal and marshmallows. Press on bottom of buttered 13×9-inch pan. Refrigerate until firm, about 30 minutes. Cut into bars; store refrigerated.   *Makes 3 dozen bars*

FAVORITE BUTTER COOKIES

*These crisp, tender cutout cookies can be decorated to
capture the spirit of your occasion.*

COOKIE

2½ cups all-purpose flour
  1 cup granulated sugar
  1 cup LAND O LAKES® Butter,
    softened

1 egg
1 teaspoon baking powder
2 tablespoons orange juice
1 tablespoon vanilla

FROSTING

  4 cups powdered sugar
  ½ cup LAND O LAKES® Butter,
    softened
  3 to 4 tablespoons milk

2 teaspoons vanilla
  Food coloring, colored sugars,
    flaked coconut and cinnamon
    candies for decorations

For cookie, in large mixer bowl combine all cookie ingredients. Beat at low speed, scraping bowl often, until well mixed, 1 to 2 minutes. If desired, divide dough into 3 equal portions; color ⅔ of dough with desired food colorings. Mix until dough is evenly colored. Wrap in plastic food wrap; refrigerate until firm, 2 to 3 hours.

Heat oven to 400°. On lightly floured surface, roll out dough, ⅓ at a time, to ¼-inch thickness. Cut out with cookie cutters. Place 1 inch apart on ungreased cookie sheets. If desired, sprinkle colored sugars on some of the cookies or bake and decorate later. Bake for 6 to 10 minutes or until edges are lightly browned. Remove immediately. Cool completely.

For frosting, in small mixer bowl combine powdered sugar, ½ cup butter, 3 to 4 tablespoons milk and 2 teaspoons vanilla. Beat at low speed, scraping bowl often, until fluffy, 1 to 2 minutes. Frost or decorate cookies.

Makes about 3 dozen (3-inch) cookies

DECORATING IDEAS:

Wreaths: Cut cookies with 2-inch round cookie cutter; bake as directed. Frost with green colored frosting. Color coconut green; sprinkle frosted cookies with coconut. Place 3 cinnamon candies together to resemble holly.

Christmas Trees: Color dough green; cut with Christmas tree cutter. Sprinkle with colored sugars; bake as directed.

Angels: Cut cookies with angel cookie cutter; bake as directed. Use blue frosting for dress, yellow frosting for hair and white frosting for wings, face and lace on dress.

Favorite Butter Cookies

CARAMEL CHOCOLATE PECAN BARS

Caramel and chocolate top a buttery crumb crust.

CRUST
2 cups all-purpose flour
1 cup firmly packed brown sugar
½ cup LAND O LAKES® Butter, softened

1 cup pecan halves

FILLING
⅔ cup LAND O LAKES® Butter
½ cup firmly packed brown sugar
½ cup butterscotch chips

½ cup semi-sweet real chocolate chips

Heat oven to 350°. For crust, in large mixer bowl combine flour, 1 cup brown sugar and ½ cup butter. Beat at medium speed, scraping bowl often, until well mixed and particles are fine, 2 to 3 minutes. Press on bottom of ungreased 13×9-inch baking pan. Sprinkle pecans evenly over unbaked crust.

For filling, in 1-quart saucepan combine ⅔ cup butter and ½ cup brown sugar. Cook over medium heat, stirring constantly, until mixture comes to a full boil, 4 to 5 minutes. Boil, stirring constantly, until candy thermometer reaches 242°F or small amount of mixture dropped into ice water forms a firm ball, 1 minute. Pour over pecans and crust. Bake for 18 to 20 minutes or until entire caramel layer is bubbly. Immediately sprinkle with butterscotch and chocolate chips. Allow to melt slightly, 3 to 5 minutes. Swirl chips leaving some whole for a marbled effect. Cool completely; cut into bars. *Makes 3 dozen bars*

CINNAMON 'N' SUGAR SHORTBREAD

This flaky shortbread is made extra special with a sprinkling of cinnamon and sugar.

SHORTBREAD
1¾ cups all-purpose flour
¾ cup powdered sugar
½ cup cake flour

1 cup LAND O LAKES® Butter, softened
½ teaspoon ground cinnamon

TOPPING
1 tablespoon granulated sugar

⅛ teaspoon ground cinnamon

Heat oven to 350°. For shortbread, in large bowl combine all shortbread ingredients. With fork stir together until soft dough forms. Divide dough in half. Press on bottom of 2 (9-inch) pie pans.

For topping, in small bowl stir together topping ingredients; sprinkle over shortbread. Score *each* into 8 wedges; pierce *each* wedge several times with fork. Bake for 20 to 30 minutes or until light golden brown. Cool in pan on wire rack; cut into wedges. *Makes 16 pieces*

Caramel Chocolate Pecan Bars

RASPBERRY-TOPPED POPPY SEED COOKIES

A tender butter cookie filled with poppy seed and topped with raspberry preserves.

1 cup LAND O LAKES® Butter,
    softened
½ cup sugar
1 egg

2 cups all-purpose flour
1 tablespoon poppy seed
½ cup raspberry preserves*

Heat oven to 350°. In large mixer bowl combine butter, sugar, egg, flour and poppy seed. Beat at low speed, scraping bowl often, until well mixed, 2 to 3 minutes. Shape rounded teaspoonfuls of dough into 1-inch balls. Place 2 inches apart onto greased cookie sheets. Flatten cookies to ¼-inch thickness with bottom of buttered glass dipped in sugar. Make small indentation in center of *each* cookie; fill with *about ½ teaspoon* preserves. Bake for 12 to 15 minutes or until edges are lightly browned.   *Makes about 3½ dozen cookies*

*You may substitute ½ cup of your favorite flavor preserves for the ½ cup raspberry preserves.

CHOCOLATE-DRIZZLED CHERRY BARS

The favorite combination of chocolate and cherry makes these bars delicious.

CRUMB MIXTURE
    2 cups all-purpose flour
    2 cups quick-cooking oats
1½ cups sugar

1¼ cups LAND O LAKES® Butter,
    softened

FILLING
    1 can (21 ounces) cherry fruit
        filling

1 teaspoon almond extract

TOPPING
½ cup semi-sweet real chocolate
    chips

1 tablespoon shortening

Heat oven to 350°. For crumb mixture, in large mixer bowl combine all crumb mixture ingredients. Beat at low speed, scraping bowl often, until mixture is crumbly, 1 to 2 minutes. *Reserve 1½ cups crumb mixture;* press remaining crumb mixture on bottom of ungreased 13×9-inch baking pan. Bake for 15 to 20 minutes or until edges are very lightly browned.

For filling, in same bowl stir together fruit filling and almond extract. Spread filling over warm crust; sprinkle with reserved crumb mixture. Continue baking for 27 to 32 minutes or until lightly browned.

For topping, in 1-quart saucepan combine chocolate chips and shortening. Cook over low heat, stirring occasionally, until melted, 1 to 3 minutes. Drizzle over bars. Cool completely; cut into bars.   *Makes 3 dozen bars*

CHOCOLATE NO-BAKE COOKIES

These tasty no-bake cookies are easy and quick to make.

1½ cups quick-cooking oats
½ cup flaked coconut
¼ cup chopped walnuts
¾ cup sugar

¼ cup milk
¼ cup LAND O LAKES® Butter
3 tablespoons unsweetened cocoa

In medium bowl combine oats, coconut and walnuts; set aside. In 2-quart saucepan combine sugar, milk, butter and cocoa. Cook over medium heat, stirring occasionally, until mixture comes to a full boil, 3 to 4 minutes. Remove from heat. Stir in oats mixture. Quickly drop mixture by rounded teaspoonfuls onto waxed paper. Cool completely. Store refrigerated.

Makes about 2 dozen cookies

Microwave Directions: In medium bowl combine oats, coconut and walnuts; set aside. In medium microwave-safe bowl melt butter on HIGH 50 to 60 seconds. Stir in sugar, milk and cocoa. Microwave on HIGH 1 minute; stir. Microwave on HIGH until mixture comes to a full boil, 1 to 2 minutes. Continue as directed.

APPLESAUCE RAISIN BARS

This moist and buttery applesauce bar is topped with a fluffy butter pecan frosting.

BARS
⅓ cup LAND O LAKES® Butter, softened
1 cup granulated sugar
1 egg
1½ cups all-purpose flour
1½ cups applesauce

1 teaspoon ground allspice
1 teaspoon ground cinnamon
¾ teaspoon baking soda
½ teaspoon salt
½ cup raisins

FROSTING
¼ cup LAND O LAKES® Butter, softened
2 cups powdered sugar
⅛ teaspoon ground allspice

⅛ teaspoon ground cinnamon
2 tablespoons milk
2 teaspoons vanilla
½ cup chopped pecans

Heat oven to 350°. For bars, in large mixer bowl combine ⅓ cup butter, granulated sugar and egg. Beat at medium speed, scraping bowl often, until light and fluffy, 1 to 2 minutes. Add flour, applesauce, 1 teaspoon allspice, 1 teaspoon cinnamon, baking soda and salt. Reduce speed to low; continue beating, scraping bowl often, until creamy, 2 to 3 minutes. By hand, stir in raisins. Spoon batter into greased 13×9-inch baking pan. Bake for 25 to 35 minutes or until wooden pick inserted in center comes out clean. Cool completely.

For frosting, in small mixer bowl combine all frosting ingredients *except* pecans. Beat at medium speed, scraping bowl often, until smooth, 1 to 2 minutes. By hand, fold in pecans. Frost; cut into bars.

Makes 4 dozen bars

DESSERTS

CHOCOLATE RASPBERRY TORTE

*A fudgy cake layer topped with glistening raspberry preserves and
a finishing touch of whipped cream.*

3 eggs, separated
⅛ teaspoon cream of tartar
⅛ teaspoon salt
1½ cups sugar
1 cup LAND O LAKES® Butter,
   melted
1½ teaspoons vanilla
½ cup all-purpose flour

½ cup unsweetened cocoa
3 tablespoons water
¾ cup finely chopped almonds
⅓ cup raspberry preserves
1 cup whipping cream, whipped,
   sweetened
Fresh raspberries

Heat oven to 350°. Grease 9-inch round cake pan. Line with aluminum foil leaving excess aluminum foil over edges; grease aluminum foil. Set aside. In small mixer bowl combine egg whites, cream of tartar and salt. Beat at high speed, scraping bowl often, until soft peaks form, 1 to 2 minutes; set aside. In large mixer bowl combine egg yolks, sugar, butter and vanilla. Beat at medium speed, scraping bowl often, until well mixed, 1 to 2 minutes. Add flour, cocoa and water. Continue beating, scraping bowl often, until well mixed, 1 to 2 minutes. By hand, stir in chopped almonds. Fold beaten egg whites into chocolate mixture. Spread into prepared pan. Bake for 40 to 55 minutes or until wooden pick inserted in center comes out clean. Cool on wire rack 1 hour; remove from pan by lifting aluminum foil. Cover; refrigerate until completely cooled, 2 to 3 hours.

To serve, remove aluminum foil; place on serving plate. Spread raspberry preserves on top. Pipe sweetened whipped cream to form a lattice top; garnish with raspberries.   *Makes 12 servings*

Chocolate Raspberry Torte

TOASTED PECAN SAUCE

The richness of butter and the crunch of toasted pecans make this sauce reminiscent of pecan pie.

½ cup sugar
⅓ cup LAND O LAKES® Butter
1 cup light corn syrup

1 egg, slightly beaten
1 tablespoon vanilla
1 cup pecan halves, toasted

In 2-quart saucepan combine sugar, butter, corn syrup, egg and vanilla. Cook over medium heat, stirring constantly, until mixture comes to a full boil, 6 to 8 minutes. Just before serving, stir in pecans. Serve warm or cool over ice cream, cake, pancakes or waffles. Store refrigerated.   *Makes 2 cups*

Microwave Directions: In 2-quart microwave-safe casserole combine sugar, butter and corn syrup. Microwave on HIGH 2 minutes; mix well. Stir 1 tablespoon hot sugar mixture into beaten egg. Slowly stir egg mixture and vanilla into hot sugar mixture. Microwave on HIGH, stirring every minute, until mixture comes to a full boil, 3 to 4 minutes. Microwave on HIGH 1 minute. Just before serving, stir in pecans. Serve warm or cool over ice cream, cake, pancakes or waffles. Store refrigerated.

CREAMY MINT FUDGE SAUCE

In just 15 minutes, this rich, minty fudge sauce is ready to top your favorite ice cream.

½ cup sugar
¼ cup LAND O LAKES® Butter
⅓ cup water
2 tablespoons light corn syrup

1 package (6 ounces) semi-sweet
   real chocolate chips (1 cup)
2 tablespoons creme de menthe*

In 2-quart saucepan combine sugar, butter, water and corn syrup. Cook over medium heat, stirring constantly, until mixture comes to a full boil, 5 to 8 minutes. Boil 3 minutes; remove from heat. Immediately add chocolate chips; beat with wire whisk or rotary beater until smooth. Stir in creme de menthe. Serve warm over ice cream or cake.   *Makes 1½ cups*

Microwave Directions: In 2-quart microwave-safe casserole combine sugar, butter, water and corn syrup. Microwave on HIGH, stirring after half the time, until mixture comes to a full boil, 3½ to 4½ minutes. Boil 2 minutes. Immediately add chocolate chips; beat with wire whisk or rotary beater until smooth. Stir in creme de menthe. Serve warm over ice cream or cake.

*You may substitute 2 tablespoons of your favorite liqueur *or* 1 teaspoon mint extract for the 2 tablespoons creme de menthe.

Toasted Pecan Sauce;
Creamy Mint Fudge Sauce

CHOCOLATE CHERRY CAKE

Cherries are the jewels in this chocolate coconut crowned cake.

CAKE

2 jars (10 ounces *each*) maraschino
   cherries, drained, *reserve juice*
2 eggs, separated
2 cups sugar
⅔ cup LAND O LAKES® Butter,
   softened
2 squares (1 ounce *each*)
   unsweetened chocolate,
   melted

3 cups all-purpose flour
2 teaspoons baking soda
½ teaspoon salt
   Reserved cherry juice plus
   enough *buttermilk* to equal
   2 cups

FROSTING

1 cup milk
3 tablespoons all-purpose flour
½ teaspoon salt
1 cup sugar

1 cup LAND O LAKES® Butter,
   softened
1 teaspoon vanilla
1 cup flaked coconut

Heat oven to 350°. For cake, cut maraschino cherries in half; set aside. In small mixer bowl beat egg whites at high speed, scraping bowl often, until soft peaks form, 1 to 2 minutes; set aside. In large mixer bowl combine egg yolks, 2 cups sugar, ⅔ cup butter and chocolate. Beat at medium speed, scraping bowl often, until well mixed, 1 to 2 minutes. In medium bowl stir together 3 cups flour, baking soda and ½ teaspoon salt. Continue beating chocolate mixture, adding flour mixture alternately with cherry juice and buttermilk mixture, until smooth, 1 to 2 minutes. By hand, fold in cherries, then egg whites. Pour into 3 greased and floured 9-inch round cake pans. Bake for 30 to 35 minutes or until wooden pick inserted in center comes out clean. Cool 5 minutes; remove from pans. Cool completely.

For frosting, in 1-quart saucepan combine milk, 3 tablespoons flour and ½ teaspoon salt. Cook over medium heat, stirring constantly, until mixture thickens and comes to a full boil, 5 to 7 minutes. Boil 1 minute. Cover surface with plastic wrap; cool completely. In small mixer bowl combine 1 cup sugar, 1 cup butter and vanilla. Beat at medium speed, scraping bowl often, until light and fluffy, 1 to 2 minutes. Beat at medium speed, gradually adding cooled flour mixture and scraping bowl often, until light and fluffy, 4 to 5 minutes. Frost between layers and entire cake. Sprinkle top and sides of cake with coconut.

Makes 12 servings

Tip: You may substitute 3 (8-inch) round cake pans for the 3 (9-inch) round cake pans. Bake for 35 to 40 minutes or until wooden pick inserted in center comes out clean.

OLD-FASHIONED BREAD PUDDING WITH VANILLA SAUCE

Warm your heart with memories while enjoying this old-fashioned bread pudding.

PUDDING

4 cups cubed white bread	½ cup granulated sugar
½ cup raisins	2 eggs, slightly beaten
2 cups milk	½ teaspoon ground nutmeg
¼ cup LAND O LAKES® Butter	1 teaspoon vanilla

VANILLA SAUCE

½ cup granulated sugar	½ cup LAND O LAKES® Butter
½ cup firmly packed brown sugar	1 teaspoon vanilla
½ cup whipping cream	

Heat oven to 350°. For pudding, in large bowl combine bread and raisins. In 1-quart saucepan combine milk and ¼ cup butter. Cook over medium heat until butter is melted, 4 to 7 minutes. Pour milk mixture over bread; let stand 10 minutes. Stir in remaining pudding ingredients. Pour into greased 1½-quart casserole. Bake for 40 to 50 minutes or until set in center.

For Vanilla Sauce, in 1-quart saucepan combine ½ cup granulated sugar, brown sugar, whipping cream and ½ cup butter. Cook over medium heat, stirring occasionally, until mixture thickens and comes to a full boil, 5 to 8 minutes. Stir in 1 teaspoon vanilla. Serve sauce over warm pudding. Store refrigerated.

Makes 6 servings

RASPBERRY CRUMBLE TART

Raspberry preserves peek from a rich, buttery crumble to make a simple but elegant dessert.

2 cups all-purpose flour	½ cup raspberry *or* favorite flavor
¾ cup granulated sugar	preserves
¾ cup LAND O LAKES® Butter, softened	1 teaspoon grated lemon peel
3 egg yolks	Powdered sugar
1 teaspoon vanilla	Fresh raspberries
½ cup coarsely chopped blanched almonds *or* pine nuts	Sweetened whipped cream

Heat oven to 350°. In large mixer bowl combine flour, granulated sugar, butter, egg yolks and vanilla. Beat at low speed, scraping bowl often, until well mixed, 2 to 3 minutes. By hand, stir in almonds. *Reserve 1½ cups mixture; set aside.* Press remaining mixture on bottom of ungreased 9-inch removable bottom tart pan. Bake 10 minutes. Spread preserves to within ½ inch from edge; sprinkle with lemon peel. Crumble reserved mixture over preserves. Continue baking for 30 to 35 minutes or until lightly browned. Cool completely; remove from tart pan. Sprinkle with powdered sugar. Serve with fresh raspberries and sweetened whipped cream.

Makes 10 to 12 servings

CHOCOLATE HAZELNUT
TRUFFLE DESSERT

Serve a thin slice of this rich, dense chocolate dessert with a creamy custard sauce.

TRUFFLE DESSERT
1 cup whipping cream
¼ cup LAND O LAKES® Butter
2 bars (8 ounces *each*) semi-sweet
    chocolate
4 egg yolks

¾ cup powdered sugar
3 tablespoons rum *or* orange juice
1 cup coarsely chopped hazelnuts
    or filberts, toasted

CUSTARD
1 cup whipping cream
¼ cup granulated sugar
1 teaspoon cornstarch

3 egg yolks
1 teaspoon vanilla

For truffle dessert, in 2-quart saucepan combine 1 cup whipping cream, butter and chocolate. Cook over medium heat, stirring occasionally, until chocolate is melted, 5 to 7 minutes. Whisk in 4 egg yolks, one at a time. Continue cooking, stirring constantly, until mixture reaches 160°F and thickens slightly, 3 to 4 minutes. Remove from heat; whisk in powdered sugar and rum. Stir in hazelnuts. Line 8×4-inch loaf pan with aluminum foil leaving 1 inch of aluminum foil over *each* edge. Pour chocolate mixture into prepared pan. Freeze 8 hours or overnight.

For custard, in 2-quart saucepan cook 1 cup whipping cream over medium heat until it just comes to a boil, 4 to 6 minutes. Remove from heat. Meanwhile, in medium bowl combine granulated sugar and cornstarch. Whisk in 3 egg yolks until mixture is light and creamy, 3 to 4 minutes. Gradually whisk hot cream into beaten egg yolks. Return mixture to saucepan; stir in vanilla. Cook over medium heat, stirring constantly, until custard reaches 160°F and is thick enough to coat back of metal spoon, 4 to 5 minutes. (Do not boil because egg yolks will curdle.) Refrigerate 8 hours or overnight.

To serve, remove truffle dessert from pan using aluminum foil to lift out. Remove aluminum foil. Slice truffle dessert with hot knife into 16 slices. Spoon about 1 tablespoon custard onto individual dessert plates; place slice of truffle dessert over custard. *Makes 16 servings*

Chocolate Hazelnut Truffle Dessert

LACE COOKIE ICE CREAM CUPS

Elegant lace cookie cups hold a scoop of your favorite ice cream.

½ cup light corn syrup
½ cup LAND O LAKES® Butter
1 cup all-purpose flour
½ cup firmly packed brown sugar
1 package (2½ ounces) slivered
    almonds, finely chopped
    (½ cup)

Semi-sweet real chocolate
    chips,* melted
Your favorite ice cream

Heat oven to 300°. In 2-quart saucepan over medium heat bring corn syrup to a full boil, 2 to 3 minutes. Add butter; reduce heat to low. Continue cooking, stirring occasionally, until butter melts, 3 to 5 minutes. Remove from heat. Stir in flour, brown sugar and almonds. Drop tablespoonfuls of dough 4 inches apart onto greased cookie sheets. Bake for 11 to 13 minutes or until cookies bubble and are golden brown. *Cool 1 minute on cookie sheets.* Working quickly, remove and shape cookies over inverted small custard cups to form cups. Cool completely; remove from custard cups.

For *each* cup, spread 1 tablespoon melted chocolate on outside bottom and 1 inch up outside edge of *each* cooled cookie cup. Refrigerate, chocolate side up, until hardened, about 30 minutes. Just before serving, fill *each* cup with large scoop of ice cream. If desired, drizzle with additional melted chocolate.

Makes 2 dozen cookie cups

*A 6-ounce (1 cup) package chocolate chips will coat 8 to 9 cookie cups, using 1 tablespoon chocolate per cup.

Tip: Make desired number of cups. With remaining dough, bake as directed above *except* shape into cones or leave flat. Serve as cookies.

DOUBLE FUDGE BROWNIE
BAKED ALASKA

A classic dessert with a new twist—chocolate in all three layers.

BROWNIES
¾ cup firmly packed brown sugar
½ cup LAND O LAKES® Butter,
    softened
¾ cup all-purpose flour

1½ cups semi-sweet miniature real
    chocolate chips, melted
3 eggs

FILLING
½ gallon chocolate-flavored ice
    cream, softened

MERINGUE
6 egg whites
¼ teaspoon salt
1 teaspoon vanilla

¾ cup granulated sugar
½ cup semi-sweet miniature real
    chocolate chips

Heat oven to 350°. Grease 9-inch round cake pan. Line with aluminum foil leaving excess aluminum foil over edges; grease aluminum foil. Set aside.

For brownies, in large mixer bowl combine brown sugar and butter. Beat at medium speed, scraping bowl often, until smooth, 2 to 3 minutes. Add flour, melted chocolate and eggs. Continue beating, scraping bowl often, until well mixed, 2 to 3 minutes. Pour into prepared pan. Bake for 40 to 50 minutes or until wooden pick inserted halfway between edge and center comes out clean. Cool completely; remove from pan by lifting aluminum foil.

For filling, line 2½-quart bowl with aluminum foil; pack ice cream into bowl. Cover; freeze until firm, 3 to 4 hours.

Heat oven to 450°. For meringue, in large mixer bowl beat egg whites at high speed, scraping bowl often, until soft peaks form, 1 to 2 minutes. Add salt and vanilla. Continue beating, gradually adding granulated sugar, until stiff peaks form, 2 to 3 minutes. Fold in ½ cup chocolate chips.

To assemble, place brownies on ovenproof plate. Invert ice cream onto brownies; remove bowl and aluminum foil. Spread meringue evenly over entire surface, covering any holes. Bake for 3 to 5 minutes or until lightly browned. Serve immediately. *Makes 12 servings*

CHERRY HEART CHEESECAKE

A decorative ring of hearts adds a sweet touch to this rich cheesecake.

CRUST

1⅓ cups crushed chocolate wafer
    cookies

¼ cup LAND O LAKES® Butter,
    melted

2 tablespoons sugar

FILLING

4 eggs, separated

½ cup LAND O LAKES® Butter,
    softened

2 packages (8 ounces) cream
    cheese, softened

1 cup sugar

1 tablespoon cornstarch

1 teaspoon baking powder

1 tablespoon lemon juice

TOPPING

1 carton (8 ounces) dairy
    sour cream (1 cup)

2 tablespoons sugar

1 teaspoon vanilla

1 can (21 ounces) cherry pie
    filling

3 tablespoons cherry flavored
    liqueur

Heat oven to 325°. For crust, in small bowl stir together all crust ingredients. Press crumb mixture on bottom of 9-inch springform pan. Bake 10 minutes; cool.

For filling, in small mixer bowl beat egg whites at high speed, scraping bowl often, until soft peaks form, 1 to 2 minutes; set aside. In large mixer bowl combine ½ cup butter, cream cheese and egg yolks. Beat at medium speed, scraping bowl often, until smooth and creamy, 2 to 3 minutes. Add 1 cup sugar, cornstarch, baking powder and lemon juice. Continue beating, scraping bowl often, until well mixed, 1 to 2 minutes. By hand, fold in beaten egg whites. Spoon filling into prepared pan. Bake for 60 to 80 minutes or until center is set and firm to the touch. (Cheesecake surface will be slightly cracked.) Cool 15 minutes; loosen sides of cheesecake from pan by running knife around inside of pan. Cool completely. (Cheesecake center will dip slightly upon cooling.)

For topping, in small bowl stir together sour cream, 2 tablespoons sugar and vanilla. Spread evenly over top of cheesecake. Spoon out 2 to 3 tablespoons of cherry sauce from pie filling; drop by teaspoonfuls onto sour cream topping. Carefully pull knife or spatula through cherry sauce forming hearts. Cover; refrigerate 4 hours or overnight. In medium bowl stir together remaining pie filling and liqueur. Serve over slices of cheesecake. Store refrigerated.

Makes 10 servings

Cherry Heart Cheesecake

GINGERBREAD WITH FRUITED COMPOTE

Winter fruits simmer with fresh gingerroot for a warm accompaniment
to this moist gingerbread.

GINGERBREAD

1¾ cups all-purpose flour
⅓ cup firmly packed brown sugar
½ cup LAND O LAKES® Butter,
   softened
½ cup light molasses
½ cup buttermilk
1 egg

1 teaspoon baking soda
½ teaspoon salt
¼ teaspoon ground nutmeg
¼ teaspoon ground cloves
2 teaspoons grated fresh
   gingerroot*
1 teaspoon grated lemon peel

FRUIT COMPOTE

2 tablespoons LAND O LAKES®
   Butter
1½ cups cored, sliced ⅛ inch tart
   cooking apple (1 large)
1½ cups cored, sliced ⅛ inch ripe
   red pear (1 large)

½ cup orange marmalade
2 teaspoons grated lemon peel
1 teaspoon lemon juice
1 teaspoon grated fresh
   gingerroot**
1 orange, pared, sectioned

Heat oven to 350°. For gingerbread, in large mixer bowl combine all ginger-bread ingredients. Beat at low speed, scraping bowl often, until well mixed, 1 to 2 minutes. Pour into greased and floured 9-inch round cake pan. Bake for 30 to 40 minutes or until top springs back when touched lightly in center. Let stand 15 minutes.

For Fruit Compote, in 2-quart saucepan melt 2 tablespoons butter until sizzling. Add apple, pear, marmalade, 2 teaspoons lemon peel, lemon juice and 1 teaspoon gingerroot. Cook over medium heat, stirring occasionally, until fruit is crisply tender, 3 to 4 minutes. (Compote sauce will be thin.) Stir in orange sections. Serve with warm gingerbread. *Makes 9 servings*

*You may substitute ½ teaspoon ground ginger for the 2 teaspoons grated fresh gingerroot.

**You may substitute ¼ teaspoon ground ginger for the 1 teaspoon grated fresh gingerroot.

CHOCOLATE PECAN PIE

Chocolate and pecan candies were the inspiration for this pie.

9-inch unbaked pie shell
⅔ cup sugar
⅓ cup LAND O LAKES® Butter,
   melted
1 cup light corn syrup

3 eggs
½ teaspoon salt
1 cup pecan halves
½ cup semi-sweet chocolate chips
Sweetened whipped cream

Heat oven to 375°. In small mixer bowl combine sugar, butter, corn syrup, eggs and salt. Beat at medium speed, scraping bowl often, until well mixed, 1 to 2 minutes. By hand, stir in pecans and chocolate chips. Pour into pie shell. Cover edge of crust with 2-inch strip of aluminum foil to prevent excess browning. Bake for 15 minutes. Remove aluminum foil; continue baking for 15 to 25 minutes or until filling is set. If desired, serve with sweetened whipped cream. *Makes 8 servings*

DATELAVA

The traditional Greek dessert Baklava takes on a new flavor with dates.

FILLING
2 cups finely chopped walnuts
¾ cup granulated sugar
2 packages (8 ounces *each*) pitted
   dates, finely chopped

1½ to 1¾ cups LAND O LAKES®
   Butter, melted
1 pound frozen phyllo dough,
   thawed

SYRUP
½ cup granulated sugar
¾ cup orange juice

½ cup honey

GLAZE
¾ cup powdered sugar

1 tablespoon milk

Heat oven to 325°. For filling, in large bowl stir together walnuts, ¾ cup granulated sugar and dates; set aside. Brush 15×10×1-inch jelly roll pan with butter. Layer 8 phyllo sheets in pan, brushing *each* with butter. Sprinkle with 2 cups filling mixture. Top with 4 more phyllo sheets, brushing *each* with butter. Repeat layering filling mixture and 4 phyllo sheets twice. Top with remaining 8 phyllo sheets, brushing *each* with butter. Cut diagonally through first phyllo layer to make diamond shapes. Bake for 60 to 70 minutes or until golden brown.

For syrup, in 2-quart saucepan combine all syrup ingredients. Cook over medium heat, stirring often, until mixture comes to a full boil, 4 to 5 minutes. Reduce heat to low; simmer until slightly thickened, 30 to 40 minutes. Pour syrup over warm dessert.

For glaze, in small bowl stir together glaze ingredients until smooth. Drizzle over dessert. *Makes 3 dozen pieces*

Tip: If sheets of phyllo dough are larger than pan, trim to fit.

CANDIES

SUGAR & SPICE PECANS   *Good*

One handful is not enough of these crunchy nuts—you'll be back for more.

¼ cup LAND O LAKES® Butter
3 cups pecan halves
½ cup sugar
3 tablespoons sugar

1 tablespoon ground cinnamon
½ teaspoon ground ginger
½ teaspoon ground nutmeg

doesn't melt well .? Karo .

In 10-inch skillet melt butter; stir in pecans and ½ cup sugar. Cook over medium heat, stirring occasionally, until sugar melts and pecans brown, 8 to 12 minutes. Meanwhile, in large bowl combine all remaining ingredients. Stir in caramelized pecans. Spread on waxed paper; cool completely. Break clusters into individual pecans. Store in tightly covered container.   *Makes 3 cups*

CREAMY NUT DIPPED CANDIES

Nuts are hidden inside these dipped coconut buttercreams.

5 cups powdered sugar
¾ cup flaked coconut
⅓ cup LAND O LAKES® Butter,
    softened
¼ teaspoon salt
3 tablespoons milk

2 teaspoons vanilla
1 cup mixed nuts
1 package (10 ounces) almond
    bark, vanilla *or* chocolate
    candy coating

In large mixer bowl combine *4 cups* powdered sugar, coconut, butter, salt, milk and vanilla. Beat at medium speed, scraping bowl often, until light and fluffy, 4 to 5 minutes. By hand, knead in remaining 1 cup powdered sugar. (Dough may be soft.) Form 1 teaspoon of dough around *each* nut; roll into ball. Refrigerate until firm, 2 hours. In 2-quart saucepan over low heat, melt almond bark. Dip chilled balls into melted coating; place on waxed paper. If desired, drizzle with remaining almond bark to decorate. Store refrigerated.

Makes about 5½ dozen candies

Sugar & Spice Pecans;
Creamy Nut Dipped Candies

RASPBERRY CREME SQUARES

*Raspberry and chocolate are layered with a rich butter cream
to form these sweet delights.*

CRUST
1¼ cups graham cracker crumbs
¼ cup granulated sugar

½ cup LAND O LAKES® Butter,
melted

FILLING
2 cups powdered sugar
¼ cup LAND O LAKES® Butter,
softened
1 package (3 ounces) cream
cheese, softened

½ teaspoon vanilla
¼ cup raspberry preserves
1 square (1 ounce) unsweetened
chocolate, melted

For crust, in medium bowl stir together all crust ingredients. Press on bottom
of buttered 9-inch square pan. Refrigerate 15 minutes.

For filling, in small mixer bowl combine powdered sugar, ¼ cup butter, cream
cheese and vanilla. Beat at medium speed, scraping bowl often, until light and
fluffy, 3 to 4 minutes. Spread over crust; spread preserves over filling. Swirl
with knife. Drizzle with melted chocolate. Cover; refrigerate until firm, 2 to 3
hours. Cut into squares. Store refrigerated.   *Makes 4 dozen candies*

MICROWAVE PEANUT BUTTER FUDGE

*The ease of microwaving and the goodness of peanut butter
make this fudge a sure winner.*

⅔ cup LAND O LAKES® Butter
⅔ cup crunchy-style peanut butter
6 cups powdered sugar

⅓ cup milk
1 tablespoon vanilla

In large microwave-safe bowl place butter and peanut butter. Microwave on
HIGH until butter melts, 1½ to 2 minutes; stir until blended. Stir in all remaining ingredients until lumps of sugar disappear. Microwave on HIGH until
softened but not bubbly, 1 to 1½ minutes; stir. Pour into buttered 9-inch square
baking pan. Cover; refrigerate at least 1 hour. Cut into squares; store
refrigerated.   *Makes 3 dozen pieces*

TOFFEE CARDAMOM NUTS

This simple to make toasted nut mixture has a hint of cardamom for a special flavor.

⅓ cup LAND O LAKES® Butter
⅓ cup light corn syrup
½ teaspoon ground cardamom

2 cups pecan halves
¾ cup blanched whole almonds
½ cup whole hazelnuts *or* filberts

Heat oven to 400°. In 15×10×1-inch jelly roll pan melt butter in oven for 4 to 5 minutes. Stir in all remaining ingredients. Bake for 15 to 18 minutes or until almonds are golden brown. Stir mixture immediately after removing from oven. *Makes 4 cups*

ALMOND BUTTER CRUNCH

This toffee candy is filled with almonds and covered with chocolate.

¾ cup LAND O LAKES® Butter
⅔ cup sugar
⅓ cup light corn syrup

1 cup blanched whole almonds
¾ cup semi-sweet real chocolate chips

In 10-inch skillet melt butter over medium heat. Stir in sugar, corn syrup and almonds. Continue cooking, stirring constantly, until almonds pop and mixture is golden brown in color, 8 to 12 minutes. Pour into 15×10×1-inch jelly roll pan. Sprinkle chocolate chips over candy; spread evenly. Cool completely; break into pieces. Store in tightly covered container. *Makes 1½ pounds*

CHOCOLATE NUT TOFFEE

*This homemade favorite, better than the candy store version,
is topped with chocolate and walnuts.*

1 cup sugar
1 cup LAND O LAKES® Butter
1 package (6 ounces) semi-sweet
  real chocolate chips (1 cup)

¼ cup chopped walnuts

In 2-quart saucepan combine sugar and butter. Cook over low heat, stirring occasionally, until candy thermometer reaches 300°F or small amount of mixture dropped into ice water forms brittle strands, 25 to 30 minutes. Spread on waxed paper lined 15×10×1-inch jelly roll pan. Sprinkle chocolate chips over hot candy; let stand 5 minutes. Spread melted chocolate evenly over candy; sprinkle with nuts. Cool completely; break into pieces. *Makes 1¼ pounds*

NAPOLEON CRÈMES

Three layers—a chocolate crumb crust, a buttercream filling and a chocolate frosting—combine to make a sinfully delicious candy.

CRUMB MIXTURE
- ¾ cup LAND O LAKES® Butter
- ¼ cup granulated sugar
- ¼ cup unsweetened cocoa
- 1 teaspoon vanilla
- 2 cups graham cracker crumbs

FILLING
- 2 cups powdered sugar
- ½ cup LAND O LAKES® Butter, softened
- 1 package (3½ ounces) instant vanilla pudding mix
- 3 tablespoons milk

FROSTING
- 1 package (6 ounces) semi-sweet real chocolate chips (1 cup)
- 2 tablespoons LAND O LAKES® Butter

For crumb mixture, in 2-quart saucepan combine ¾ cup butter, granulated sugar, cocoa and vanilla. Cook over medium heat, stirring occasionally, until butter melts, 5 to 6 minutes. Remove from heat. Stir in crumbs. Press on bottom of buttered 9-inch square pan; cool.

For filling, in small mixer bowl combine all filling ingredients. Beat at medium speed, scraping bowl often, until smooth, 1 to 2 minutes. Spread over crust; refrigerate until firm, about 30 minutes.

For frosting, in 1-quart saucepan melt frosting ingredients over low heat; spread over bars. Cover; refrigerate until firm, about 1 hour. Cut into squares; store refrigerated.   *Makes 64 candies*

PEANUT BUTTER CANDIES

The popular flavors of peanut butter and chocolate team up in this easy-to-make candy.

- 1 cup LAND O LAKES® Butter
- 1 cup crunchy-style peanut butter
- 2 cups powdered sugar
- 2 cups graham cracker crumbs
- 1 package (6 ounces) semi-sweet real chocolate chips (1 cup), melted

In 2-quart saucepan melt butter and peanut butter. Stir in powdered sugar and graham cracker crumbs. Shape rounded teaspoonfuls of mixture into 1-inch balls. Place on waxed paper. Make a depression in center of *each* ball with back of teaspoon. Fill *each* depression with ½ teaspoon melted chocolate. Store refrigerated.   *Makes about 5 dozen candies*

Napoleon Crèmes

BUTTERY PEANUT BRITTLE

Wrap Buttery Peanut Brittle in plastic wrap and tie with a colorful ribbon for a great gift idea.

2 cups sugar
1 cup light corn syrup
½ cup water
1 cup LAND O LAKES® Butter,
   cut into pieces

2 cups raw Spanish peanuts
1 teaspoon baking soda

In 3-quart saucepan combine sugar, corn syrup and water. Cook over low heat, stirring occasionally, until sugar is dissolved and mixture comes to a full boil, 20 to 30 minutes. Add butter; continue cooking, stirring occasionally, until candy thermometer reaches 280°F or small amount of mixture dropped into ice water forms a pliable strand, 80 to 90 minutes. Stir in peanuts; continue cooking, stirring constantly, until candy thermometer reaches 305°F or small amount of mixture dropped into ice water forms a brittle strand, 12 to 14 minutes. Remove from heat; stir in baking soda. Pour mixture onto 2 buttered cookie sheets; spread about ¼ inch thick. Cool completely; break into pieces.

Makes 2 pounds

BUTTERY PECAN CARAMELS

These buttery caramels are topped with a crown of chocolate and a crunchy pecan half.

2 cups sugar
2 cups half-and-half (1 pint)
¾ cup light corn syrup
½ cup LAND O LAKES® Butter

½ cups semi-sweet real chocolate
   chips, melted
64 pecan halves

In 4-quart saucepan combine sugar, *1 cup* half-and-half, corn syrup and butter. Cook over medium heat, stirring occasionally, until mixture comes to a full boil, 7 to 8 minutes. Add remaining 1 cup half-and-half; continue cooking, stirring often, until candy thermometer reaches 245°F or small amount of mixture dropped into ice water forms a firm ball, 35 to 40 minutes. Pour into buttered 8-inch square pan. Cover; refrigerate 1 to 1½ hours to cool. Cut into 64 pieces. Drop ¼ teaspoon melted chocolate on top of *each* caramel; press pecan half into chocolate. Cover; store refrigerated.

Makes 64 caramels

Buttery Peanut Brittle;
Buttery Pecan Caramels

FOR THE HOLIDAYS

ORANGE SPICED GINGERBREAD CUTOUTS

These old-fashioned gingerbread cookies are fun to make.

COOKIES
⅓ cup firmly packed brown sugar
⅓ cup LAND O LAKES® Butter, softened
⅔ cup light molasses
1 egg

2 teaspoons grated orange peel
2¾ cups all-purpose flour
1 teaspoon ground ginger
½ teaspoon baking soda
½ teaspoon salt

FROSTING
4 cups powdered sugar
½ cup LAND O LAKES® Butter, softened

3 to 4 tablespoons milk
2 teaspoons vanilla
Food coloring

For cookies, in large mixer bowl combine brown sugar, ⅓ cup butter, molasses, egg and orange peel. Beat at medium speed, scraping bowl often, until smooth and creamy, 1 to 2 minutes. Add all remaining cookie ingredients. Reduce speed to low. Continue beating, scraping bowl often, until well mixed, 1 to 2 minutes. Cover; refrigerate at least 2 hours.

Heat oven to 375°. On well floured surface, roll out dough, half at a time (keeping remaining dough refrigerated), to ¼-inch thickness. Cut with 3- to 4-inch cookie cutters. Place 1 inch apart on greased cookie sheets. Bake for 6 to 8 minutes or until no indentation remains when touched. Remove immediately. Cool completely.

For frosting, in small mixer bowl combine powdered sugar, ½ cup butter, 3 to 4 tablespoons milk and vanilla. Beat at low speed, scraping bowl often, until fluffy, 1 to 2 minutes. If desired, color frosting with food coloring. Decorate cookies with frosting. *Makes about 4 dozen cookies*

Orange Spiced Gingerbread Cutouts;
Holiday Chocolate Butter Cookies (page 72)

HOLIDAY CHOCOLATE BUTTER COOKIES

A rich, chocolate butter cookie with endless possibilities.

½ cup sugar
¾ cup LAND O LAKES® Butter, softened
1 egg yolk
1 teaspoon almond extract
1½ cups all-purpose flour
¼ cup unsweetened cocoa
   Semi-sweet real chocolate chips, melted *or* vanilla-flavored candy coating, melted for coatings

Finely chopped almonds, pecans *or* walnuts; candy coated milk chocolate pieces; flaked coconut; fruit preserves; colored sugars and multi-colored decorator candies for toppings

Heat oven to 375°. In large mixer bowl combine sugar, butter, egg yolk and almond extract. Beat at medium speed, scraping bowl often, until mixture is light and fluffy, 2 to 3 minutes. Continue beating, gradually adding flour and cocoa, until well mixed, 2 to 3 minutes. Shape rounded teaspoonfuls of dough into 1-inch balls. Place 1 inch apart on ungreased cookie sheets. Shape as desired (logs; flatten with sugar dipped, buttered glass; thumbprint or depression in center; etc.). Bake for 7 to 9 minutes or until set. Cool completely. Decorate cookies with suggested coatings and toppings, as desired.

Makes about 3 dozen cookies

Tip: Food coloring and flavor extracts can be added to vanilla-flavored candy coating, if desired.

CRANBERRY APPLE COBBLER

Sugar glazed cranberries and apples peek through a sweet, crisp cobbler topping.

COBBLER
½ cup all-purpose flour
½ cup granulated sugar
½ cup firmly packed brown sugar
½ teaspoon ground cinnamon
½ teaspoon ground nutmeg

4 cups peeled, cored, sliced ¼ inch thick, tart cooking apples (4 medium)
2 cups fresh *or* frozen whole cranberries, thawed

CRUMB TOPPING
⅔ cup all-purpose flour
½ cup granulated sugar

½ cup LAND O LAKES® Butter
Ice cream

Heat oven to 400°. For cobbler, in large bowl combine ½ cup flour, ½ cup granulated sugar, brown sugar, cinnamon and nutmeg. Add apples and cranberries; toss to coat with flour mixture. Place in 2-quart casserole.

For crumb topping, in medium bowl stir together ⅔ cup flour and ½ cup granulated sugar; cut in butter until crumbly. Sprinkle over fruit mixture. Bake for 40 to 45 minutes or until golden brown. Serve warm with ice cream.

Makes 8 servings

HOLIDAY NUT CARAMEL CORN

Wrap this festive caramel corn for a fun gift.

20 cups popped popcorn
2 cups firmly packed brown
  sugar
1 cup LAND O LAKES® Butter
½ cup light corn syrup
½ teaspoon salt

½ teaspoon baking soda
2 cups salted cashews,
  macadamia nuts *or* pistachio
  nuts
6 ounces chocolate- *or* vanilla-
  flavored candy coating

Heat oven to 200°. In roasting pan place popcorn; set aside. In 3-quart sauce-pan combine brown sugar, butter, corn syrup and salt. Cook over medium heat, stirring occasionally, until mixture comes to a full boil, 12 to 14 minutes. Continue cooking, stirring occasionally, until candy thermometer reaches 238°F or small amount of mixture dropped in ice water forms a soft ball, 4 to 6 minutes. Remove from heat; stir in baking soda. Pour over popcorn; sprinkle cashews over caramel mixture. Stir until popcorn is coated. Bake for 20 minutes; stir. Continue baking 25 minutes. Remove from oven; immediately spread caramel corn on waxed paper. In 1-quart saucepan melt candy coating over low heat, stirring occasionally, until smooth, 3 to 5 minutes. Drizzle candy coating over caramel corn; cool completely. Break into pieces; store in tightly covered container. *Makes 18 cups*

Tip: Two cups candy coated milk chocolate pieces *or* raisins can be stirred into caramel corn immediately after removing from oven.

GOLDEN PUMPKIN BREAD

A spicy version of a popular quick bread.

1½ cups all-purpose flour
1 cup firmly packed brown sugar
1 cup cooked mashed pumpkin*
½ cup LAND O LAKES® Butter,
  softened
2 eggs

1½ teaspoons ground cinnamon
1 teaspoon baking powder
1 teaspoon baking soda
1 teaspoon salt
½ teaspoon ground ginger
¼ teaspoon ground cloves

Heat oven to 350°. In large mixer bowl combine all ingredients. Beat at medium speed, scraping bowl often, until well mixed, 2 to 3 minutes. Pour into greased 9×5-inch loaf pan or 3 greased 5½×3-inch mini-loaf pans. Bake for 45 to 55 minutes for 9×5-inch loaf or 30 to 35 minutes for mini loaves, or until wooden pick inserted in center comes out clean. Cool 10 minutes; remove from pan. Cool completely; store refrigerated. *Makes 1 (9×5-inch) loaf or 3 mini loaves*

*You may substitute 1 cup canned pumpkin for 1 cup cooked pumpkin.

PECAN PUMPKIN TORTE

The festive flavors of pumpkin, pecans and spices create this showcase torte.

CAKE

2 cups crushed vanilla wafers
1 cup chopped pecans
¾ cup LAND O LAKES® Butter, softened
1 package (18 ounces) spice cake mix

1 can (16 ounces) solid-packed pumpkin
¼ cup LAND O LAKES® Butter, softened
4 eggs

FILLING

3 cups powdered sugar
⅔ cup LAND O LAKES® Butter, softened
4 ounces cream cheese, softened

2 teaspoons vanilla
¼ cup caramel topping
Pecan halves

Heat oven to 350°. For cake, in large mixer bowl combine wafer crumbs, 1 cup chopped pecans and ¾ cup butter. Beat at medium speed, scraping bowl often, until crumbly, 1 to 2 minutes. Press mixture evenly on bottom of 3 greased and floured 9-inch round cake pans. In same bowl combine cake mix, pumpkin, ¼ cup butter and eggs. Beat at medium speed, scraping bowl often, until well mixed, 2 to 3 minutes. Spread 1¾ cups batter over crumbs in *each* pan. Bake for 20 to 25 minutes or until wooden pick inserted in center comes out clean. Cool 5 minutes; remove from pans. Cool completely.

For filling, in small mixer bowl combine powdered sugar, ⅔ cup butter, cream cheese and vanilla. Beat at medium speed, scraping bowl often, until light and fluffy, 2 to 3 minutes. On serving plate layer 3 cakes, nut side down, with ½ cup filling spread between *each* layer. With remaining filling, frost sides only of cake. Spread caramel topping over top of cake, drizzling some over the frosted sides. Arrange pecan halves in rings on top of cake. Store refrigerated.

Makes 16 servings

Tip: To remove cake easily from pan, place wire rack on top of cake and invert; repeat with remaining layers.

Pecan Pumpkin Torte

JEWELED CHEESE BALL

This make-ahead cheese ball is studded with sweet dates and rolled in almonds.

2 cups (8 ounces) shredded
    Cheddar cheese
1 cup chopped pitted dates
½ cup LAND O LAKES® Butter,
    softened

1 tablespoon brandy*
½ cup toasted sliced almonds
    Assorted crackers

In small mixer bowl combine Cheddar cheese, dates, butter and brandy. Beat at medium speed, scraping bowl often, until well mixed. Cover; refrigerate at least 1 hour. Shape mixture into large ball; roll in toasted almonds. Cover; refrigerate at least 1 hour. Remove from refrigerator ½ hour before serving. Serve with assorted crackers.   *Makes 1 cheese ball*

*You may substitute ¼ teaspoon brandy extract for the 1 tablespoon brandy.

CHOCOLATE COVERED
SURPRISE COOKIES

Chocolate frosting hides cherries nestled in these chocolate cookies.

COOKIES
¾ cup sugar
¾ cup LAND O LAKES® Butter,
    softened
1 egg
1½ teaspoons vanilla
1¾ cups all-purpose flour
⅓ cup unsweetened cocoa

¼ teaspoon baking powder
¼ teaspoon baking soda
⅛ teaspoon salt
1 jar (10 ounces) maraschino
    cherries, drained, *reserve*
    juice, halved

FROSTING
1 package (6 ounces) semi-sweet
    real chocolate chips (1 cup)

2 tablespoons reserved cherry
    juice

Heat oven to 350°. For cookies, in large mixer bowl combine sugar and butter. Beat at medium speed, scraping bowl often, until well mixed, 1 to 2 minutes. Add egg and vanilla; continue beating until well mixed, 1 to 2 minutes. Add flour, cocoa, baking powder, baking soda and salt. Beat at low speed, scraping bowl often, until well mixed, 1 to 2 minutes. Shape into 1-inch balls. Place 1 inch apart on ungreased cookie sheets. Press cherry half into center of *each* cookie. Bake for 8 to 10 minutes or until set. Cool completely.

For frosting, in 1-quart saucepan combine frosting ingredients. Cook over low heat, stirring occasionally, until chocolate chips melt and frosting is smooth, 4 to 5 minutes. Frost cherry on *each* cookie. Refrigerate until set. Store cookies tightly covered.   *Makes about 3½ dozen cookies*

Jeweled Cheese Ball

GRAMMIE'S PFEFFERNUSSE

These dime-size cookies, flavored with anise, disappear by the handful.

¼ cup boiling water
2 tablespoons anise seed
3½ cups all-purpose flour
⅔ cup sugar

⅔ cup LAND O LAKES® Butter, softened
⅔ cup dark corn syrup
½ teaspoon baking soda

In large mixer bowl combine boiling water and anise seed; let stand 20 minutes. Add all remaining ingredients. Beat at low speed, scraping bowl often, until well mixed, 3 to 4 minutes. Cover; refrigerate until firm, 2 to 3 hours. On lightly floured surface roll portions of dough into ropes ½ inch in diameter. Place ropes on waxed paper lined cookie sheet; cover. Refrigerate ropes until firm, 1 to 2 hours.

Heat oven to 350°. Cut ropes into ⅜-inch slices. Place ½ inch apart on un-greased cookie sheets. Bake for 8 to 10 minutes or until very lightly browned around edges.
Makes about 28 dozen dime-size cookies

ORANGE CRANBERRY BREAD

Festive cranberries are accented with a touch of orange in this quick bread.

BREAD

½ cup LAND O LAKES® Butter, softened
¾ cup granulated sugar
1 egg
1 teaspoon grated orange peel
2½ cups all-purpose flour
⅔ cup orange juice

⅓ cup milk
2 teaspoons baking powder
½ teaspoon salt
¾ cup coarsely chopped fresh *or* frozen cranberries
⅓ cup chopped pecans

GLAZE

1 cup powdered sugar

3 to 4 teaspoons orange juice

Heat oven to 350°. For bread, in large mixer bowl combine butter, granulated sugar, egg and orange peel. Beat at medium speed, scraping bowl often, until well mixed, 1 to 2 minutes. Reduce speed to low. Add flour, ⅔ cup orange juice, milk, baking powder and salt. Continue beating, scraping bowl often, until well mixed, 1 to 2 minutes. By hand, stir in cranberries and pecans. Spoon into greased 9×5-inch loaf pan or 3 greased 5½×3-inch mini-loaf pans. Bake for 50 to 60 minutes for 9×5-inch loaf or 30 to 40 minutes for mini loaves, or until wooden pick inserted in center comes out clean. Cool 10 minutes; remove from pan. Cool completely.

For glaze, in small bowl stir together glaze ingredients; spread over cooled bread.
Makes 1 (9×5-inch) loaf or 3 mini loaves

JULEKAGE
(Fruit Bread)

This festive round bread is filled with candied fruit, raisins and almonds.

BREAD

1 package (¼ ounce) active dry
    yeast
¼ cup warm water (105° to 115°F)
3¼ to 3¾ cups all-purpose flour
½ cup golden raisins
⅓ cup slivered almonds
⅓ cup mixed, chopped candied
    fruit
¼ cup granulated sugar

¾ cup milk
¼ cup LAND O LAKES® Butter,
    softened
1 egg
½ teaspoon salt
½ teaspoon ground cardamom
½ teaspoon grated lemon peel
    LAND O LAKES® Butter,
    melted

GLAZE

1 cup powdered sugar
3 to 4 teaspoons milk

Candied cherries

For bread, in large mixer bowl dissolve yeast in warm water. Add 2 *cups* flour, raisins, almonds, candied fruit, granulated sugar, ¾ cup milk, ¼ cup butter, egg, salt, cardamom and lemon peel. Beat at medium speed, scraping bowl often, until smooth, 1 to 2 minutes. By hand, stir in enough remaining flour to make dough easy to handle. Turn dough onto lightly floured surface; knead until smooth and elastic, about 5 minutes. Place in greased bowl; turn greased side up. Cover; let rise in warm place until double in size, about 1½ hours. Dough is ready if indentation remains when touched. Punch down dough; shape into round loaf. Place in greased 9-inch round cake pan. Brush top of bread with melted butter. Cover; let rise in warm place until double in size, about 1 hour.

Heat oven to 350°. Bake for 35 to 45 minutes or until golden brown. Remove immediately from pan. Cool completely.

For glaze, in bowl stir together powdered sugar and 3 to 4 teaspoons milk. Spread over bread. If desired, garnish with candied cherries. *Makes 1 loaf*

JAN HAGEL

This traditional Scandinavian bar just melts in your mouth.

2 cups all-purpose flour
1 cup sugar
1 cup LAND O LAKES® Butter,
    softened

1 egg, separated
1 teaspoon ground cinnamon
½ teaspoon salt
1 cup sliced almonds

Heat oven to 350°. In large mixer bowl combine flour, sugar, butter, egg yolk, cinnamon and salt. Beat at low speed, scraping bowl often, until well mixed, 2 to 3 minutes. Divide dough in half. Press *each* half onto an ungreased cookie sheet to ¹⁄₁₆-inch thickness. In small bowl beat egg white with fork until foamy. Brush over dough; sprinkle with almonds. Bake for 12 to 15 minutes or until very lightly browned. Immediately cut into 2-inch squares and remove from pan. Cool; store in tightly covered container. *Makes 3 to 4 dozen cookies*

APRICOT CARDAMOM WREATH

Brandied apricots are tucked inside a sweet cardamom bread, which is shaped in a wreath and sprinkled with sugar crystals.

BREAD

1 cup granulated sugar	¼ cup warm water (105° to 115°F)
1 teaspoon ground cardamom	½ cup dairy sour cream
½ cup LAND O LAKES® Butter	3 eggs
1 can (12 ounces) evaporated milk	6 to 7 cups all-purpose flour
2 teaspoons salt	
2 packages (¼ ounce *each*) active dry yeast	

FILLING

2 to 2½ cups water	1 egg, slightly beaten
¼ cup brandy *or* water	2 tablespoons milk
1 package (6 ounces) dried apricots (2 cups)	Large crystal sugar

For bread, in 2-quart saucepan stir together granulated sugar and cardamom; add butter, evaporated milk and salt. Cook over medium heat, stirring occasionally, until butter is melted, 5 to 8 minutes. Cool to warm (105° to 115°F). In large mixer bowl dissolve yeast in ¼ cup warm water; stir in warm milk mixture, sour cream, 3 eggs and *3 cups* flour. Beat at medium speed, scraping bowl often, until smooth, 1 to 2 minutes. By hand, stir in enough remaining flour to make dough easy to handle. Turn dough onto lightly floured surface; knead until smooth and elastic, about 5 minutes. Place in greased bowl; turn greased side up. Cover; let rise in warm place until double in size, about 1 to 1½ hours. Dough is ready if indentation remains when touched.

For filling, in 2-quart saucepan combine *2 cups* water, brandy and apricots. Cook over low heat, stirring occasionally and adding small amounts of additional water, if necessary, until apricots are tender and mixture is thickened, 40 to 45 minutes; set aside.

Punch down dough; divide in half. Let rest 10 minutes. On lightly floured surface roll one half of dough to 20×9-inch rectangle; cut into 3 (3-inch-wide) strips. Spread *each* strip with ¼ *cup* apricot mixture to within ½ inch of edges. Bring 20-inch sides up together; pinch sides and ends tightly to seal well. Gently braid filled strips together. Place on greased large cookie sheet; form into wreath or leave as a braid. Pinch ends to seal well. Repeat with remaining dough and apricot mixture. Cover; let rise in warm place 30 minutes.

Heat oven to 350°. Bake for 25 to 30 minutes or until lightly browned. (Cover with aluminum foil if bread browns too quickly.) In small bowl stir together beaten egg and 2 tablespoons milk. Brush breads with egg mixture; sprinkle with large crystal sugar. Continue baking for 5 to 10 minutes or until golden brown. Remove from cookie sheets; cool on wire racks. *Makes 2 wreaths*

Tip: For best results, bake 1 wreath at a time.

Apricot Cardamom Wreath

RICH CHOCOLATE FUDGE

This rich, velvety chocolate fudge can be made three ways—Macadamia Nut, Rocky Road or Apricot.

FUDGE

4 cups sugar
½ cup LAND O LAKES® Butter
1 can (12 ounces) evaporated milk
1 package (12 ounces) semi-sweet real chocolate chips (2 cups)

3 bars (4 ounces *each*) sweet baking chocolate
1 jar (7 ounces) marshmallow cream
2 teaspoons vanilla

VARIATIONS

Macadamia Nut
1¼ cups coarsely chopped macadamia nuts

Rocky Road
1¼ cups coarsely chopped walnuts, toasted
30 marshmallows (3 cups), cut into quarters

Apricot
1¼ cups coarsely chopped dried apricots

In 4-quart saucepan combine sugar, butter and evaporated milk. Cook over medium-high heat, stirring occasionally, until mixture comes to a full boil, 10 to 14 minutes. Reduce heat to medium; boil, stirring constantly, until candy thermometer reaches 228°F or small amount of mixture dropped into ice water forms a 2-inch soft thread, 6 to 7 minutes. Remove from heat, gradually stir in chocolate chips and chocolate until melted. Stir in marshmallow cream and vanilla until well blended.

For Macadamia Nut Fudge, stir in *1 cup* nuts. Spread into buttered 13×9-inch pan. Sprinkle with remaining ¼ cup nuts.

For Rocky Road Fudge, stir in *1 cup* nuts, then stir in marshmallows, leaving marbled affect. Spread into buttered 13×9-inch pan. Sprinkle with remaining ¼ cup nuts.

For Apricot Fudge, stir in apricots. Spread into buttered 13×9-inch pan.

Cool completely at room temperature. Cut into 1-inch squares. Store covered in cool place.

Makes about 9 to 10 dozen pieces

Right to left: Rocky Road Fudge; Apricot Fudge; Macadamia Nut Fudge

DANISH KRINGLE

This tender Danish pastry is filled with the richness of almond paste, brown sugar and butter.

COFFEE CAKE

2¼ cups all-purpose flour
2 tablespoons granulated sugar
½ teaspoon salt
½ cup LAND O LAKES® Butter
1 package (¼ ounce) active dry yeast

¼ cup warm water (105° to 115°F)
½ cup whipping cream
1 egg

FILLING

1 package (7 ounces) almond paste
¼ cup firmly packed brown sugar

¼ cup LAND O LAKES® Butter, softened

GLAZE

1 cup powdered sugar
3 to 5 teaspoons milk
¼ teaspoon almond extract

Sliced almonds
Candied cherries

For coffee cake, in large bowl combine flour, granulated sugar and salt; cut in ½ cup butter until crumbly. Dissolve yeast in warm water. Stir yeast, whipping cream and egg into flour mixture. Cover; refrigerate until dough is firm, 2 to 4 hours.

For filling, in small mixer bowl combine all filling ingredients. Beat at medium speed, scraping bowl often, until well mixed, 1 to 2 minutes; set aside.

Divide dough in half. Return half to refrigerator. On lightly floured surface roll *half* of dough into 15×6-inch rectangle. Spread *half* of filling lengthwise down center of rectangle in 2-inch strip. Fold sides of dough over filling pinching to seal well; pinch ends to seal well. Place coffee cake seam side down on greased cookie sheet in the shape of a horseshoe. Repeat with remaining dough and filling. Cover; let rise in warm place 30 minutes.

Heat oven to 375°. Bake for 13 to 23 minutes or until golden brown. Cool completely.

For glaze, in small bowl stir together powdered sugar, 3 to 5 teaspoons milk and almond extract. Spread over cooled coffee cakes. If desired, garnish with sliced almonds and candied cherries. *Makes 2 coffee cakes*

Tip: For best results, bake one coffee cake at a time.

SANDBAKKELS
(Sugar Cookie Tarts)

Small sandbakkel molds are used to make these delicate Scandinavian cookie tarts.

½ cup granulated sugar
½ cup firmly packed brown sugar
1 cup LAND O LAKES® Butter, softened

1 egg
1 teaspoon almond extract
2½ cups all-purpose flour

Heat oven to 350°. In large mixer bowl combine granulated sugar, brown sugar, butter, egg and almond extract. Beat at medium speed, scraping bowl often, until well mixed, 1 to 2 minutes. Reduce speed to low; add flour. Continue beating, scraping bowl often, until well mixed, 2 to 3 minutes. If dough is too soft, refrigerate until firm, 1 to 2 hours. Press 2 to 3 teaspoons dough into *each* sandbakkel mold. Place molds on cookie sheets. Bake for 8 to 11 minutes or until lightly browned. Cool 5 minutes; remove from molds by tapping on table or loosening with knife. Cookies can be served plain or if desired, fill with fresh fruit, fruit filling, pudding or sweetened whipped cream.

Makes about 3 dozen cookies

Tip: You may substitute mini-muffin pans for the sandbakkel molds. Press 1 tablespoon dough into *each* cup. Bake as directed above.

FRUIT-FILLED THUMBPRINTS

These tender butter cookies are rolled in nuts and filled with fruit preserves.

2 cups all-purpose flour
½ cup firmly packed brown sugar
1 cup LAND O LAKES® Butter, softened
2 eggs, separated

⅛ teaspoon salt
1 teaspoon vanilla
1½ cups finely chopped pecans
Fruit preserves

Heat oven to 350°. In large mixer bowl combine flour, brown sugar, butter, egg yolks, salt and vanilla. Beat at low speed, scraping bowl often, until well mixed, 2 to 3 minutes. Shape rounded teaspoonfuls of dough into 1-inch balls. In small bowl beat egg whites with a fork until foamy. Dip *each* ball of dough into egg whites; roll in chopped pecans. Place 1 inch apart on greased cookie sheets. Make a depression in center of *each* cookie with back of a teaspoon. Bake for 8 minutes; remove from oven. Fill centers with preserves. Continue baking for 6 to 10 minutes or until lightly browned.

Makes about 3 dozen cookies

SLOVAKIAN KOLACKY

Kolacky—a tender, buttery pastry filled with fruit preserves. Absolutely delicious!

2 packages (¼ ounce *each*) active
    dry yeast
¼ cup warm water (105° to 115°F)
7 cups all-purpose flour
1 teaspoon salt

2 cups LAND O LAKES® Butter,
    softened
4 eggs, slightly beaten
2 cups whipping cream (1 pint)
Fruit preserves

In small bowl dissolve yeast in warm water. In large bowl combine flour and salt; cut in butter until crumbly. Stir in yeast, eggs and whipping cream. Turn dough onto lightly floured surface; knead until smooth, 2 to 3 minutes. Place in greased bowl; turn greased side up. Cover; refrigerate until firm, 6 hours or overnight.

Heat oven to 375°. Roll out dough, ½ at a time, on sugared surface to ⅛-inch thickness. Cut into 3-inch squares. Spoon 1 teaspoon preserves in center of *each* square. Bring up two opposite corners to center; pinch together tightly to seal. Fold sealed tip to one side; pinch to seal. Place 1-inch apart on ungreased cookie sheets. Bake for 10 to 15 minutes or until lightly browned.

Makes 5 dozen kolacky

CHOCOLATE SNOWBALLS

A moist, chocolate version of popular Russian tea cakes.

¾ cup firmly packed brown sugar
¾ cup LAND O LAKES® Butter
¼ cup milk
3 squares (1 ounce *each*)
    unsweetened chocolate,
    melted
1 egg

1 teaspoon vanilla
2 cups all-purpose flour
1 cup chopped nuts
1 teaspoon baking powder
½ teaspoon salt
¼ teaspoon baking soda
Powdered sugar

Heat oven to 350°. In large mixer bowl combine brown sugar and butter. Beat at medium speed, scraping bowl often, until light and fluffy, 1 to 2 minutes. Add milk, melted chocolate, egg and vanilla. Continue beating, scraping bowl often, until well mixed, 1 to 2 minutes. Reduce speed to low. Add flour, nuts, baking powder, salt and baking soda. Continue beating, scraping bowl often, until well mixed, 1 to 2 minutes. Cover and refrigerate until firm, 1 to 2 hours. Shape rounded teaspoonfuls of dough into 1-inch balls. Place 2 inches apart on ungreased cookie sheets. Bake for 8 to 10 minutes or until set. Carefully remove from cookie sheets. Roll in powdered sugar while still warm and again when cool.

Makes about 5 dozen cookies

Slovakian Kolacky

FRUITED STREUSEL KUCHEN WITH ORANGE CREAM

Sliced apples, cranberries, dried fruits and nuts combine with sugar to form a streusel topping on this orange-flavored cake.

KUCHEN

2¼ cups all-purpose flour
2 teaspoons baking powder
¼ teaspoon salt
⅓ cup sugar
⅓ cup LAND O LAKES® Butter, softened
2 eggs
½ cup milk
½ cup orange juice
1 tablespoon orange-flavored liqueur *or* orange juice

1 teaspoon vanilla
1 large tart cooking apple, peeled, cored, sliced ⅛ inch thick
½ cup coarsely chopped dried apricots
½ cup dried figs, quartered
½ cup golden raisins
½ cup coarsely chopped walnuts
½ cup fresh *or* frozen whole cranberries

STREUSEL TOPPING

½ cup sugar
2 tablespoons LAND O LAKES® Butter, softened

1 teaspoon ground cinnamon
1 teaspoon grated orange peel

ORANGE CREAM

2 cups whipping cream (1 pint)
¼ cup sugar
2 teaspoons grated orange peel

1 tablespoon orange-flavored liqueur *or* orange juice

Heat oven to 350°. For Kuchen, in medium bowl stir together flour, baking powder and salt; set aside. In large mixer bowl beat together ⅓ cup sugar and ⅓ cup butter at medium speed, scraping bowl often, until well mixed, 1 to 2 minutes. Continue beating, adding eggs 1 at a time, until well mixed, 1 to 2 minutes. Reduce speed to low. Continue beating, scraping bowl often and gradually adding flour mixture alternately with milk and ½ cup orange juice, until smooth, 2 to 3 minutes. By hand, stir in 1 tablespoon orange-flavored liqueur and vanilla. Spread into greased 12½-inch removable bottom tart pan. Arrange apple slices around outside edge of surface. Sprinkle apricots, figs, raisins, walnuts and cranberries around and on top of apple slices. Gently press into batter.

For streusel topping, in medium bowl stir together all streusel topping ingredients; sprinkle over fruit. Bake for 35 to 45 minutes or until lightly browned.

For Orange Cream, in small chilled mixer bowl beat chilled whipping cream at high speed, scraping bowl often, until soft peaks form, 1 to 2 minutes. Continue beating, gradually adding ¼ cup sugar and 2 teaspoons orange peel, until stiff peaks form. By hand, fold in 1 tablespoon orange-flavored liqueur. Serve with warm Kuchen.   *Makes 12 servings*

Fruited Streusel Kuchen with Orange Cream

BEST EVER SPRITZ   *average*

The best ever recipe for buttery spritz with 5 festive variations.

⅔ cup sugar (less?)   ½ teaspoon salt
1 cup LAND O LAKES® Butter,   2 teaspoons vanilla
   softened   2¼ cups all-purpose flour
1 egg

Heat oven to 400°. In large mixer bowl combine sugar, butter, egg, salt and vanilla. Beat at medium speed, scraping bowl often, until mixture is light and fluffy, 2 to 3 minutes. Add flour. Beat at low speed, scraping bowl often, until well mixed, 2 to 3 minutes. If desired, add the ingredients from one of the following variations. If dough is too soft, cover; refrigerate until firm enough to form cookies, 30 to 45 minutes. Place dough into cookie press; form desired shapes 1 inch apart on ungreased cookie sheets. Bake for 6 to 8 minutes or until edges are lightly browned.   *Makes about 5 dozen cookies*

VARIATIONS:

Lebkuchen Spice Spritz: To Best Ever Spritz dough add *1 teaspoon* each *ground cinnamon* and *ground nutmeg, ½ teaspoon ground allspice* and *¼ teaspoon ground cloves.* Glaze: In small bowl stir together *1 cup powdered sugar, 2 tablespoons milk* and *½ teaspoon vanilla* until smooth. Drizzle or pipe over warm cookies.

Eggnog Glazed Spritz: To Best Ever Spritz dough add *1 teaspoon ground nutmeg.* Glaze: In small bowl stir together *1 cup powdered sugar; ¼ cup LAND O LAKES® Butter, softened; 2 tablespoons water* and *¼ teaspoon rum extract* until smooth. Drizzle over warm cookies.

Piña Colada Spritz: Omit vanilla in Best Ever Spritz recipe above and add *1 tablespoon pineapple juice* and *¼ teaspoon rum extract;* stir in *½ cup finely chopped coconut.* Frosting: In small mixer bowl combine *1 cup powdered sugar; 2 tablespoons LAND O LAKES® Butter, softened; 2 tablespoons pineapple preserves* and *1 tablespoon pineapple juice.* Beat at medium speed, scraping bowl often, until light and fluffy, 2 to 3 minutes. Spread on cooled cookies. If desired, sprinkle with *toasted coconut.*

Mint Kisses: To Best Ever Spritz dough add *¼ teaspoon mint extract.* Immediately after removing cookies from oven place *1 chocolate candy kiss* on *each* cookie.

Chocolate Chip Spritz: To Best Ever Spritz dough add *¼ cup coarsely grated semi-sweet chocolate.*

Lebkuchen Spice Spritz;
Brandied Buttery Wreaths (page 92)

BRANDIED BUTTERY WREATHS

This rich, buttery cookie is delicately flavored with brandy and nutmeg.

COOKIES
2¼ cups all-purpose flour
⅓ cup granulated sugar
⅔ cup LAND O LAKES® Butter,
   softened
1 egg
1 teaspoon ground nutmeg

¼ teaspoon salt
2 tablespoons grated orange peel
2 tablespoons brandy*
⅓ cup chopped maraschino
   cherries, drained

GLAZE
1¼ cups powdered sugar
1 to 2 tablespoons milk
1 tablespoon brandy**

⅛ teaspoon ground nutmeg
Red and green maraschino
   cherries, drained, halved

Heat oven to 350°. For cookies, in large mixer bowl combine flour, granulated sugar, butter, egg, 1 teaspoon nutmeg, salt, orange peel and 2 tablespoons brandy. Beat at low speed, scraping bowl often, until well mixed, 1 to 2 minutes. By hand, stir in ⅓ cup chopped cherries. Shape rounded teaspoonfuls of dough into 1-inch balls; form into 5-inch long strips. Shape strips into circles (wreaths), candy canes *or* leave as strips. Place 2 inches apart on greased cookie sheets. Bake for 8 to 12 minutes or until edges are lightly browned.

For glaze, in small bowl stir together all glaze ingredients *except* halved maraschino cherries. Dip or frost warm cookies with glaze. If desired, decorate with maraschino cherries. *Makes about 2 dozen cookies*

 *You may substitute 1 teaspoon brandy extract *plus* 2 tablespoons water for the 2 tablespoons brandy.

**You may substitute ¼ teaspoon brandy extract *plus* 1 tablespoon water for the 1 tablespoon brandy.

SNOWBALL COOKIES

A favorite at Christmas time, pecan-filled Snowball Cookies
are scrumptious all year 'round.

2 cups all-purpose flour
2 cups finely chopped pecans
¼ cup granulated sugar
1 cup LAND O LAKES® Butter,
   softened

1 teaspoon vanilla
Powdered sugar

Heat oven to 325°. In large mixer bowl combine flour, pecans, granulated sugar, butter and vanilla. Beat at low speed, scraping bowl often, until well mixed, 3 to 4 minutes. Shape rounded teaspoonfuls of dough into 1-inch balls. Place 1 inch apart on ungreased cookie sheets. Bake for 18 to 25 minutes or until very lightly browned. Remove immediately. Roll in powdered sugar while still warm and again when cool. *Makes about 3 dozen cookies*

CHOCOLATE STEAMED PUDDING

This elegant cake-like pudding is easy to make.

¾ cup all-purpose flour
¾ cup granulated sugar
½ cup LAND O LAKES® Butter, softened
3 eggs
¼ cup half-and-half

3 tablespoons unsweetened cocoa
⅛ teaspoon salt
½ teaspoon vanilla
Powdered sugar
Sweetened whipped cream *or* chocolate sauce

In small mixer bowl combine flour, granulated sugar, butter, eggs, half-and-half, cocoa, salt and vanilla. Beat at medium speed, scraping bowl often, until well mixed, 3 to 4 minutes. Pour into well greased 1-quart metal mold or casserole. Place a double thickness of greased waxed paper on top, then cover with double thickness of aluminum foil. Tie tightly with heavy string. Trim paper and aluminum foil leaving about 1 inch overhang.

Place rack in Dutch oven or roasting pan; add boiling water to just below rack. Place mold on rack. Bring water to a full boil; cover with lid. Reduce heat to medium; continue cooking over simmering water for 2 hours or until center springs back when touched lightly. Add boiling water occasionally to keep water level just below rack. Remove from Dutch oven; let stand 2 to 3 minutes.

To serve, remove covers and unmold. Dust generously with powdered sugar. Serve warm or cold. If desired, serve with sweetened whipped cream or chocolate sauce. *Makes 8 servings*

BUTTERY FRUIT CAKE

This buttery pound cake, filled with candied fruit, is especially nice during the holiday season.

2¼ cups all-purpose flour
1½ cups sugar
1 cup LAND O LAKES® Butter, softened
1 package (8 ounces) cream cheese, softened

4 eggs
1½ teaspoons baking powder
1½ teaspoons vanilla
1½ cups candied fruit mix
½ cup chopped walnuts

Heat oven to 350°. In large mixer bowl combine *1¼ cups* flour, sugar, butter, cream cheese, eggs, baking powder and vanilla. Beat at medium speed, scraping bowl often, until well mixed, 2 to 3 minutes. By hand, stir in remaining 1 cup flour, candied fruit and nuts. Pour into 2 greased and floured 8×4-inch loaf pans or 6 greased and floured 5½×3-inch mini-loaf pans. Bake 8×4-inch loaves for 50 to 60 minutes or mini loaves for 45 to 55 minutes, or until wooden pick inserted in center comes out clean. Cool 10 minutes; remove from pans. Cool completely. *Makes 2 (8×4-inch) loaves or 6 mini loaves*

INDEX